DATE DUE

Workers' Compensation Benefits: Adequacy, Equity, and Efficiency

John D. Worrall and
David Appel, editors

ILR Press
New York State School of
Industrial and Labor Relations
Cornell University

The research on which this volume is based was originally
funded by the National Council
on Compensation Insurance. The
council's assistance is gratefully
acknowledged.

Cover design by Kathleen Dalton

Library of Congress number: 85-8208
ISBN: 0-87546-115-8

Library of Congress Cataloging in Publication Data
Workers' compensation benefits.

   Bibliography: p.
   Includes index.
   1. Workers' compensation—United States—Addresses,
essays, lectures.   I. Worall, John D.   II. Appel, David,
1950-
HD7103.65.U6W663   1985   368.4'1'00973   85-8208
ISBN 0-87546-115-8

Copies may be ordered from
ILR Press
New York State School of
Industrial and Labor Relations
Cornell University
Ithaca, NY 14853

Printed in the United States of America by Braun-Brumfield
5   4   3   2   1

CONTENTS

TABLES

FIGURES

1 · SOME BENEFIT ISSUES IN WORKERS' COMPENSATION

John D. Worrall and David Appel

More than two million families a year receive cash benefits from the workers' compensation program (Worrall 1982), and the current payroll cost of cash and medical benefits is over 25 billion dollars a year. Recent program costs and an index of how benefits have grown over time are presented in table 1.1. Why has this program grown and survived? Have increasing benefit levels affected the behavior of employees and employers? What role has the government played in the growth process? A group of economists has examined some of the benefit issues in the compensation of workers for injuries and diseases "arising out of and in the course" of employment. This volume contains their essays delivered at the Second Annual Seminar on Economic Issues in Workers' Compensation held at the Graduate Center of the City College of New York, on November 19, 1982, under the sponsorship of the National Council on Compensation Insurance.

The National Council on Compensation Insurance is the primary actuarial, research, and rate-making organization for workers' compensation insurance in the United States. The Council has been a center for actuarial research for decades; to encourage economic

We thank Philip Borba, John F. Burton, Jr., Richard J. Butler, James Chelius, Stuart Dorsey, Sally Fillmore, William G. Johnson, Janet P. Moran, Robert S. Smith, two anonymous referees, and the editors of ILR Press for helpful comments on the papers in this volume. The usual disclaimers apply.

research in the area of workers' compensation and related social insurance programs, the Council formed an economic and social research division in 1979, and sponsored a seminar series beginning in the autumn of 1981. The result of the first seminar, *Safety and the Work Force: Incentives and Disincentives in Workers' Compensation,* was published by the ILR Press in 1983. The results of the second are presented in this volume.

A Framework for Evaluating Benefit Issues

Economists have used the concepts of adequacy, equity, and efficiency to examine the workers' compensation and related social insurance programs. Berkowitz (1973), for example, sets out some of the adequacy and equity criteria for evaluating workers' compensation income benefits. Equity issues address questions of fairness, such as: Are injured workers receiving a high enough percentage of lost wages as compensation for their injuries? Are the minimum benefits paid under the workers' compensation laws sufficient to meet a minimum standard of living? Are two people with the same pre-injury wage and with the identical injury and residual impairment receiving the same workers' compensation benefits? Is a worker with higher pre-injury wages and a more severe job injury receiving a higher benefit than a lower paid, less severely injured worker? Benefits paid may affect the number of injuries received on the job and the number of insurance claims filed; the kinds of jobs people will take and the hours of labor they will supply; the wages employers will offer, and the numbers and kind of employees they will hire; and a host of similar efficiency issues. These issues have received significant attention in workers' compensation research in recent years. The first seminar in this series, for example, was devoted primarily to efficiency questions (see Worrall 1983).

The impact of benefit levels on efficiency can be evaluated by considering demand and supply questions. The demand and supply of labor can be modeled and the incentive issues examined using underlying choice theoretic framework. Government establishes the level, dispersion, and types of benefits paid under workers' compensation. State legislatures can alter the incentives to employers and employees and affect economic efficiency. Government also ultimately determines the adequacy and equity of benefits. The papers in this volume deal with adequacy, equity, and the efficiency effects of benefits in workers' compensation. Before we review some of the principal findings of the chapters herein, we shall set out a brief overview of the workers' compensation programs.

The Workers' Compensation Programs

A workers' compensation program requires employers to provide cash benefits, medical care, and rehabilitation services to their employees for injury or illness arising out of and in the course of employment.[1] The workers' compensation laws are state laws, which provide for mandatory coverage in forty-seven states, with New Jersey, South Carolina, and Texas being elective states. In those three states, employers who do not elect coverage forgo their right to the common law defenses against negligence suits and, as a consequence, most employers choose coverage. Federal employees are covered by the Federal Employees Compensation Act, administered by the U.S. Department of Labor.

The system emerged with a quid pro quo. In exchange for giving up their right to tort actions, employees are to get swift and certain payment from the workers' compensation program without having to demonstrate the employer was at fault. In exchange, employers enjoy limited liability for industrial injury or disease. Seamen and railroad workers are exempt from the state workers' compensation laws by virtue of the Jones Act and the Federal Employers Liability Act, and these workers retain their right to sue their employers.

The workers' compensation system is litigious in some states. This can erode the certainty of payment to injured workers that the system was designed to provide. Similiarly, there have been many court challenges in recent years to the workers' compensation exclusive remedy doctrine, in which employees have brought actions against employers (Larson 1982).

Employers can fulfill their obligations to provide workers' compensation coverage by purchasing insurance from a private insurance

---

1. This brief explanation of the workers' compensation system is not meant to be complete. Those who would like a fuller treatment should see National Commission on State Workmens' Compensation Laws (1973). For the seminal treatise on workers' compensation law, see Larson (1978).

carrier or from an insurance fund run by the state or by self-insuring. Eighteen states have state funds. Twelve of these compete with private insurance carriers for business and are usually referred to as competitive state funds. The other states have exclusive state funds, and private insurance carriers are not permitted to sell workers' compensation insurance in those states.

Firms that self-insure can usually do so by posting a bond or deposit of securities with the state industrial commission. Most firms are too small to meet the requirements of state law for self-insurance. Group self-insurance is permitted in some states, and firms, usually in the same industry, can jointly self-insure.[2]

Claims made by injured or diseased employees fall into five categories:

1. *Noncomp medical*, or *medical only*, claims are claims that do not involve indemnity payments. Workers' compensation provides for virtually unlimited payment of medical benefits.

2. *Temporary total disability* claims are those claims for an injury or disease that prevents someone from working but from which full recovery is expected. Workers who have temporary total disabilities draw indemnity benefits after a waiting period, three to seven days in most states. If they are incapacitated for a period longer than that established by law, typically twenty-eight days, they receive retroactive benefits for the waiting period. More serious claims are also subject to waiting and retroactive periods. Temporary total claims are three times more common than the more serious indemnity claims, but they account for only 18 or 19 percent of the indemnity cost.[3]

3. *Permanent partial disability* claims are those indemnity claims for injuries that are expected, even after a period of healing, to result

2. The U.S. Chamber of Commerce publishes the *Analysis of Workers' Compensation Laws*, an annual that details, by state, the allowable insurance arrangements, the minimum and maximum benefits, the waiting period, the retroactive period, the replacement rates, and so forth.

3. The figures given are for different policy periods by state. They provide a good guide, however, to claim and indemnity distribution. The percentages of total indemnities for the four compensable disability categories for the last policy period reported by each state were, as of April 1984: temporary total, 18.8 percent; permanent partial, 64.9 percent; permanent total, 8.9 percent; and death, 7.4 percent. These calculations exclude Nevada, North Dakota, Ohio, Washington, and West Virginia entirely, as well as the state funds for Montana and Utah.

in a permanent impairment, functional limitation, or loss of earning capacity. Permanent partial claimants usually experience a period of temporary total disability. Permanent partial claims can be classified as major or minor claims, depending on the severity of the injury and indemnity claim, and as a group, these claims are by far the most costly in the workers' compensation system. They account for 65 percent of indemnity costs.

4. *Permanent total disability* claims are those resulting from injuries or diseases that prevent the worker from any work and are of permanent duration.[4] These cases are relatively rare, two to three of every thousand indemnity claims, but they account for 9 percent of indemnity costs.

5. *Death claims* are those resulting from fatal injuries or diseases. Burial and survivor benefits are paid in these cases. Death claims are slightly more common than permanent total claims, and they also account for 7 percent of indemnity costs.

Indemnity Benefits

Indemnity (cash) benefits are paid in addition to any medical expenses for temporary total, permanent partial, permanent total, and death claims. As of January 1, 1982, most states paid 66.66 percent of wages for temporary or permanent total disability. Idaho and Washington, which paid 60 percent, New Jersey and West Virginia, which paid 70.00 percent, and Iowa and Michigan, which paid 80.00 percent of spendable earnings, were the exceptions.[5]

These replacement rates are nominal. The amount replaced is subject to minimum and maximum amounts in all states. The maximums have grown dramatically, partially as a result of recommendations by the National Commission on State Workmen's Compensation Laws. Twenty-six of the states have temporary total benefit maximums of 100 percent of the statewide average weekly wage (SAWW); four states have maximums greater than 100 percent of the SAWW; and the

---

4. There are exceptions in some states, for example, the "working in pain" doctrine or the "odd lot" rule, which allow workers to work at temporary jobs or at occupations other than their normal ones.

5. Ohio paid 72.00 percent for the first twelve weeks, and 66.66 percent thereafter. See U.S. Chamber of Commerce (1981), chart 5.

remainder have maximums between 66.66 and 100.00 percent of the statewide average or a specific dollar amount. The maximums are lower for permanent total than temporary total disability in two states, Utah and Wyoming. There are limits on the length of time a worker can collect temporary total disability benefits, but they affect very few cases. There are also limits on duration of benefits for permanent and death cases. These limits affect a relatively much higher percentage of claims. Indemnity benefits are not taxable, and as a consequence of this and the minimum and maximum provisions, the real rate of wage replacement can exceed 100.00 percent, or for high-wage workers, fall short of 66.66 percent.

Lump sum settlements (also called wash outs, redemptions, compromise and release settlements) are permitted in most states. They are more common in serious cases.

Death benefits are paid in all states. They are similar to those for total disability claims, with similar replacement rates, maximums and minimums. The percentage of wage replacement is reduced, however, in some states, for surviving spouses without children.

The Price of Insurance

The price that employers pay for their workers' compensation insurance depends, among other things, on their size, experience, classification, and insurance arrangement.[6] There are about six hundred workers' compensation class codes. These are used to classify businesses according to their primary activity.

Manual rates, basically the average losses plus overhead, are based upon the experience of all firms in a given class and state. Manual rates are quoted in terms of $100 of payroll.

Firms that, on average, generate a premium of $2,500 at manual rate are subject to *mandatory experience rating*. There is some variation in this dollar amount and its date of adoption across states. In 1980, when the manual premium required for experience rating was $750, the average hourly earnings in the private sector were $6.66 (U.S. Department of Labor 1982), and workers' compensation as a

---

6. The rate-making process is a complicated one. An explanation can be found in *The Pricing of Workers' Compensation Insurance*, National Council on Compensation Insurance (1981b).

percentage of payroll was 1.94 percent. A firm paying $6.66 an hour with three full-time employees in a classification rated at $1.94 per $100 of payroll would probably have qualified for experience rating in 1980.

Firms that qualify for experience rating have their manual rate modified based on their actual—as opposed to expected—loss experience. The experience of the most recent three years is used for the calculation of the modifier. The degree of credibility assigned to a firm's experience varies directly with the size of the firm. Large firms generating $500,000 to $1,000,000 of premium are self-rated, and small firms generating $2,500 in premiums (and with lower statistical significance assigned to their experience) pay close to the group or manual rate.[7]

All firms that generate a premium of $5,000 or more are subject to mandatory *premium discounts*. The discount increases in steps with the size of the premium and is designed to capture economies of scale in overhead.

Firms that generate $5,000 of premium can also choose to purchase *a retrospective rate plan*. This option is usually chosen by larger firms. Retrospective plans are basically cost-plus insurance. The employer pays the loss costs, subject to bounds, and an insurance charge.

Finally, employers can receive dividends that substantially alter the net price of their workers' compensation insurance. In some instances, sliding scale dividend plans, based on the individual employer's losses, may be used. In others, flat rate dividend plans, the same dividend is paid to all policy holders.

Injury Trends

From 1972 to 1980 the incidence of occupational injury and illness cases involving lost workdays increased 20 and 30 percent for the private and manufacturing sectors, respectively. During the same period, lost workdays per hundred full-time workers increased by 41 and 39 percent for those sectors, and the rate for nonfatal cases without lost work time fell dramatically. What was fueling the in-

---

7. *ABC's of Experience Rating*, National Council on Compensation Insurance (1981a) provides a useful introduction to experience rating and calculation of the experience modifier.

creasing frequency and lengthening duration of these more serious and expensive cases? Were some of them cases that would have previously not involved lost workdays? Would this explain some of the decrease in the number of cases without lost work time?

The increase in the incidence of lost work time cases during the 1972–80 period came on the heels of a large increase in the 1960s. The Occupational Safety and Health Act (OSHA) of 1970 mandated a new and expanded annual survey of work injuries and illnesses. Data collection under the new system began in 1971, but data for only a half year are available for that year.[8] Old estimates, however, indicate that between 1960 and 1970 the incidence of injury cases increased by 27 percent in the manufacturing sector. Although the old and new incidence rate series are not comparable, two researchers have attempted to splice the series. Their results indicate that in the manufacturing sector injury frequency nearly doubled, increasing 86 percent, from 1960 to 1979 (Naples and Gordon 1981, table 1.1).

Proponents of OSHA believed that through its safety standards, inspections, and enforcement powers, the act would help to clean up the workplace and reduce job-related illnesses and injuries. Some antagonists thought that OSHA would be a costly government intrusion into relatively efficient markets. The jury is still out on OSHA's effect on job injury.[9]

Workers' Compensation Costs

The act also created the National Commission on State Workmen's Compensation Laws. The commission was charged with the responsibility of investigating the state workers' compensation laws to determine if workers were receiving adequate, prompt, and equitable compensation for job injuries or diseases. It held nine hearings and submitted its final report (National Commission on State Workmen's Compensation Laws 1973), which made 19 essential recommenda-

---

8. *Occupational Injuries and Illnesses by Industry, 1972* (U.S Department of Labor, Bureau of Labor Statistics [BLS] 1974) presents the first full year of data under the new collective system. BLS warns that the estimates for the six-month period in 1971 (published in BLS bulletin 1798) should not be compared with rates for later years.

9. See Mitchell (1982, 157) for a review of research on the labor market effects of OSHA and other federal regulation. She reports on the data problems and mixed research results, but notes that "the best available firm-level evidence indicates that current practice has a small negative effect on workplace injuries."

tions. Nine of these called for benefit changes. The U.S. Department of Labor (1981) has monitored the states' progress in complying with the essential recommendations and has found that from 1972 to 1980 states have made more progress in complying with the nine benefit recommendations than with the other recommendations.

Indeed, the rapid increase in benefits and hence employer costs during the 1970s was due in part to the commission's recommendations. From 1973, the year after the commission's report, to 1980, the cost of workers' compensation insurance rose from $1.17 to $1.96 per $100.00 of payroll, a 68 percent increase in seven years. By contrast, in the twenty-year period from 1953 to 1972, workers' compensation costs rose from $0.94 to $1.14 per $100.00 of payroll, a 21 percent increase (Price 1981). Benefits grew from an index level of 100.0 in 1972 to 154.1 in 1982, a 54 percent increase.[10]

Today, benefits increase in virtually every state in every year. Nearly all states increase benefits automatically, because their benefits are tied to their state's average weekly wage (Tinsley 1982). With increases in benefit levels, frequency and severity of injury, and increasing costs for workers' compensation came employer cries that their insurance rates were too high, regulators' demands to know why costs were rising so rapidly, and pressure on legislatures to do something.

Competition, Injuries, and Compensating Differentials

Economic theory holds that in a world of perfectly competitive markets, workers will be paid a compensating wage differential equal to the expected pecuniary and nonpecuniary value of risk borne by the marginal worker.[11] Furthermore, workers will be indifferent between buying their own insurance (the actuarially fair premium equal to the compensating differential) or the provision of workers' compensation insurance.[12] In such a world, changing the liability for injuries will not affect injury rates.

---

10. See table 1.1.

11. We are simplifying here. Such markets would be in equilibrium when the marginal gains from all occupations that the worker could hold were equal. Injury risk would be only one factor contributing to the equilibrating process. For an excellent review, see Smith (1979).

12. This implies zero transaction costs, perfect knowledge, and so forth. See Coase (1960) for the development of the Coase theorem.

Benefits that an injured worker receives make an injury less costly to the worker. To the extent that employers pay for the benefits, accidents are costly to employers. In the world of perfect markets, the optimal number of accidents would occur. As employers sought to maximize profit and workers with their various tastes and preferences for risk bearing sought to maximize their utility, the accident rates and compensating wage differentials in the various industries and occupations would be simultaneously determined. In such markets, attempts to reduce accidents below the optimal level would generate more cost than benefit. Similarly, forcing individual workers to bear less risk than they wanted to bear—and be rewarded for bearing—would reduce their satisfaction.

The chapters presented in this volume describe a world that is not perfectly competitive. It is a world in which we do not know with perfect certainty the outcome of our choices, a world in which information is costly to acquire and other transaction costs and frictions abound. Employees, employers, and governments must make choices in this world. The choices they make involve trade-offs. We turn, now, to some of what the chapters tell us about these choices and trade-offs.

Benefit Changes, Frictions, and Transaction Costs

Benefit changes have been induced by frictions and transaction costs in the workers' compensation system. Berkowitz and Berkowitz set out a historical perspective that illustrates this point. Many of the so-called threats to the workers' compensation system, including those considered by Berkowitz and Berkowitz, have arisen as a result of these costs and the concomitant divergence from the market ideal we have described above. There is much to be learned from how workers' compensation and the legal establishment have responded to these threats.

First, note that information makes markets function efficiently. If employees, employers, legislators, and insurers had perfect knowledge, much current and past controversy about workers' compensation would not exist. Berkowitz and Berkowitz indicate that the first great challenge to the workers' compensation system was the divergence between the expectations of the reformers and planners who brought the workers' compensation program to fruition and the actual program results. Their expectations were not fulfilled. They did not know the future with perfect certainty.

Uncertainty and the frictional cost associated with the delays in compensating injured workers were instrumental in the formation of the workers' compensation system. Workers were uncertain if they would receive any compensation should they be injured on the job. Employers were uncertain of their ultimate costs. The courts were the arbitrators of a de facto compensation system and the proprietors of what was, essentially, an institutional lottery.

The workers' compensation program does not exist in a vacuum. There are a panoply of programs designed to serve people with impairments or functional limitations, regardless of the work-relatedness of the impairment or limitation. The workers' compensation program, however, is a privately financed social insurance program designed to provide income maintenance. It has not been a welfare program. The Social Security Program has suffered from an insurance-welfare schizophrenia that has not plagued the workers' compensation program. The lack of ability, or desire, to attribute a disease to its occupational source allows the cost burden of death or disability to be shifted to society at large. For example, a work-induced disease that is compensated under the Social Security Disability Insurance (SSDI) program does not cause the cost of that claim to be internalized but, rather, shifts the cost to all employees and employers, or anyone who bears a general revenues tax burden.

This shifting can have perverse effects on the optimal number of injuries and illnesses. The government constitutes a major divergence from the ideal world described above. It mandates less than perfect experience rating. It sets incentives that may be less than optimal. It provides other transfer payment programs that change the opportunity cost of time for injured (and noninjured) workers and the safety incentives of employers.

There is great pressure today on the workers' compensation system in the area of occupational diseases. These claims are controverted because of a lack of knowledge of the etiology of disease and the role that work plays in the process, an inability to distinguish between fraudulent and legitimate claims, and the effects of lack of knowledge on the expected value of claims. Will the response to such uncertainty be the creation of special funds (see, in this volume, Larson and Burton). Or will occupational disease (OD), or at least specific diseases such as asbestosis, be removed from the private market as suggested by "Miller bills" (see, in this volume, Berkowitz and Berkowitz)? We are witnessing uncertainty and delay in the payment of claims. The reformers did not foresee the current OD conundrum.

The stock of knowledge increases over time. Claims that are currently being filed were not anticipated years ago. As the work-relatedness of disease is established, workers continue to file claims that were not anticipated and for which inadequate reserves may have been established. Such inadequacies could lead to strains on the system. As we become more knowledgeable, however, we will be able to attribute more claims to their legitimate source. If we are interested in maintaining an insurance mechanism, this is a desirable outcome. Similarly, increased knowledge may cause compensating differentials to be distributed differently, as workers and employers factor such information into their labor market decisions. There are different assumptions about how such information is processed by workers (see, in this volume, Dickens, and Worrall and Butler) and employers (see, in this volume, Victor, and Bartel and Thomas).

The rapid rates of inflation that ravaged the fixed benefits that were paid to permanently impaired workers were not anticipated. Chapters by Berkowitz and Berkowitz, Larson and Burton, and Williams each consider the implications of these depreciated benefits. The National Commission on State Workmen's Compensation Laws, chaired by John F. Burton, Jr., was in part a response to this phenomenon. The growth of, and continuing pressure for, benefit adjustment funds (see Larson and Burton), was another. These benefit changes have adequacy, equity, and efficiency effects.

Rationality and Efficiency Effects

A growing body of research evidence indicates that there is a positive association between workers' compensation benefits, and indemnity claim or injury report filing. Studies by Bartel and Thomas (1982), Butler (1983), Butler and Worrall (1983), Chelius (1983, 1982, 1977), Ruser (1984), and Worrall and Appel (1982) have all obtained this result. The economists who have done these research studies do not necessarily believe that large numbers of workers try to injure themselves simply to collect benefits, or file fraudulent claims to do so (Staten and Umbeck 1983, 1982) but, rather, that workers are willing to bear more risk, be less cautious, file more claims for a given accident level, or a combination of the three (see Butler 1983, or Butler and Worrall 1983, for example). Most of these studies contain implicit assumptions that employees are rational, risk-averse, expected utility maximizers. The model of employee behavior used would lead to the hypotheses that have been sustained: injuries and claims vary directly with benefits and inversely with wages.

These studies have been primarily concerned with the frequency of injury and claim filing, although some have considered the severity of claims or the duration of time in claim status as well. Worrall and Appel (1982), for example, have considered the percentage of indemnity claims filed for a given level (1,000) of "medical only" claims. They have found a significant increase in the percentage of indemnity claims as the replacement ratio, the ratio of indemnity benefits to pre-injury wages, was increased. Butler (1983) and Chelius (1983, 1982) have also considered the severity of claims, but their severity measures were contaminated because they included frequency components and claims for disability spells that were not completed. In this volume, Worrall and Butler present the first study of the severity of workers' compensation claims that takes into account nonwork spells that are incomplete and time dependence.

Worrall and Butler find that whereas higher benefits increase the duration of nonwork spells of workers with low back injuries who are temporary total disability claimants, higher wages decrease that same duration. The statistical technique that Worrall and Butler employ allows for time dependence.

Time dependence is positive if the longer one is on a claim, the more likely one is to leave claimant status in the next *very* small time interval, and negative if the longer one is on a claim the more likely one is to remain on a claim in the next *very* small time interval. Worrall and Butler observed single spells of disability for each of the claimants in their sample. Given the proportional hazard technique they used and the single-spell data with which they were working, they could not determine if the sample of claims was characterized by negative time dependence.

In a follow-up to their chapter, in which they use parametric full information maximum likelihood techniques (Butler and Worrall 1985), the main conclusion of their chapter is sustained. Claimants respond to changes in benefits and wages in the fashion hypothesized.

The less costly nonwork spells are to employees, the longer the duration one expects and observes.

The frequency and severity studies generally focus on the supply side of the labor market. They are designed as models of employee behavior. However, if benefit and wage changes affect the demand side of the labor market—namely, employers' safety incentives—these studies, particularly the frequency studies, are reduced form studies whose findings reflect the *net* effect of changes in program structure.

Very little work has been done to date on the impact of workers' compensation insurance on the demand side of the labor market. Typically, firms are considered to be profit maximizing–cost minimizing. As the degree of experience rating of firms varies under workers' compensation, the cost of a claim to a firm may vary with firm size. Chelius and Smith (1983) have attempted to test for the impact of experience rating on employer safety. They find no measurable result. However, Ruser (1984) has found that the injury rate response to benefit changes depended on the degree of experience rating. The response was stronger for smaller firms.

In his chapter, Victor uses actual workers' compensation experience to demonstrate that the safety incentive provided by experience rating can be quite substantial. His findings are important in several ways. They demonstrated the counterintuitive result that firms that are experience rated may have stronger safety incentives than firms that self-insure. They demonstrate an important efficiency consideration: full economic loss may be imposed on an experience-rated firm. They also provide the framework for future research in this area. Victor's research can lead to the ranking of firms by safety incentive. Proper modeling can effectively test employer response.

Government can affect employer safety response through mechanisms other than the workers' compensation system. One method it has used is the establishment of the OSHA, described earlier. Government can require safety investments, control noncompliance monitoring and costs, and intervene directly on the employer side of the market. As noted above, some consider OSHA to be a costly intrusion into relatively efficient markets. In this volume, Bartel and Thomas report the results of their study of the OSHA role in industrial safety investment and its benefits and costs. They found that investment in safety and health was responsive to OSHA inspections. However, they also found that the elasticity of lost workdays as a result of injury with respect to safety investment was only 2.1 percent. In other words, if employers doubled safety investment levels, the lost workday rate would fall by only 2.1 percent. They calculate the benefits and costs of safety investments induced by osha enforcement and arrive at the conclusion that the cost of such investment far outweighs the benefit. Their calculations imply that on average 1.32 cents of every dollar expended are recouped. If their calculations are correct, such an horrendous investment—a loss of 98.7 cents of every dollar—would not bode well for the efficiency effects of osha.

The standard choice theoretical framework used to formulate models of employee behavior appears to do a reasonable job of explaining economic reality. Workers are rewarded for risk bearing. Butler (1983), Butler and Worrall (1983), Dorsey (1983), Dorsey and Walzer (1983), and Smith (1979) report this result.

Workers report that they are exposed to hazards at work (Viscusi 1979b; Leigh 1982; and Worrall and Butler 1983). Those who report that they are exposed to hazards likely to lead to occupational injury or disease are more likely to file claims and to report health conditions caused by job accident or bad working conditions (Worrall and Butler 1983). Although it is the subjective measure of job risk that affects workers' supply prices, Viscusi (1979a) has found that there is a high positive correlation between such subjective measures and an objective measure, the industry injury rate. He has also found a positive relationship between job riskiness and wages controlling for other factors.

Dickens's chapter offers another explanation for the existence of compensating differentials, osha-related turnover, and differential injury rates by age. Dickens begins with an examination of the decision sequence confronting a worker in the standard neoclassical search model. He presents evidence from the psychological literature that people make systematic judgment errors, are inconsistent, and do not consider all salient information when making decisions. He then considers several simple models showing workers who are attentive and inattentive to safety. These models are capable of generating compensating differentials and can be used as an alternative to the explanation of the turnover results of the adaptive behavior model posited by Viscusi (1979c).

It is clear that workers do not have perfect knowledge. It is also the case that the future is both risky and uncertain. The manner in which employers and employees process information and formulate expectations is an important research topic. If workers are "irrational," the policy pursued by osha should be quite different than if workers are, on average or at the margin, "rational." Government provision of safety information may not be as effective as direct intervention, for example. Over 5 million individual claims are filed in a single year for job injury or disease. Although 4.5 million of these result in claims for medical expenses only, job injury is a common occurrence.

Dickens's models, which must still be developed and tested, present a different view of the world. Notice that Dickens does not claim that people are always irrational. He is not proposing that people do not respond to economic incentives, attempt to go to the best quality school given their constraints, pursue quality information, or exhibit a host of similar behaviors economists expect to see. He simply offers his models as alternative explanations of some osha behaviors.

Adequacy and Equity

Efficiency decisions are constrained. The Rehabilitation Act of 1973 mandated that priority in rehabilitation services be given to those individuals who are "most severely handicapped." This change in the law undoubtedly decreased the number of people with impairments or functional limitations who were restored to the labor market. We traded rehabilitations to achieve an equity goal. Such equity-efficiency trade-offs are common.

Larson and Burton, in their chapter, provide an analysis of special funds in workers' compensation. The frequency studies cited above provide some evidence that increasing real benefit levels or replacement rates will generate more indemnity claims and, perhaps, more serious injuries as well. Larson and Burton present a strong brief for indexing serious indemnity claimants' benefits. They do so on both adequacy and vertical equity grounds. Why should seriously injured workers bear the cost of unforeseen inflation? Do we know that they have been paid a compensating differential to bear this combined injury-inflation risk? If they have received such differentials, should we compensate them again?

Larson and Burton also analyze subsequent-, or second-injury funds. Persons with an impairment or functional limitation may face an additional barrier to employment. An employer, particularly one who is self-rated, may be reluctant to hire such a worker because a given accident is likely to result in a cumulatively greater degree of residual impairment than for a worker without a preexisting condition. Second-injury funds would shift the cost burden attributable to the preexisting disability from the hiring employer to the work community at large and remove the decrement in the hiring probability attributable to this expected cost.

Williams details the development of minimum benefits in the various states and jurisdictions in his chapter. Claimants collecting minimum benefits can have replacement rates of 100 percent or more. The injured worker can collect more (and tax free) compensation by extending his or her disability spell than by returning to work. The benefits levels established as minimums in the state provide a microcosm of the adequacy and equity questions confronting the system.

Consider the case of a highly paid, skilled, employed craftsperson who takes a low-paid part-time job after work "to help with the bills." If this person suffers a severe injury while on the part-time job, his or her income loss can be staggering. If a state and its citizens subscribe to the insurance-cost internalization-income maintenance view, this injured worker should be compensated at the minimum level. Other programs, particularly income support, should provide for this worker. If a low wage earner is injured on his or her primary job, the percentage of short-term wage loss may be zero. However, the benefit received is small, and other programs may have to provide income support. Increasing minimum benefits improves benefit adequacy, but it moves workers' compensation away from income maintenance and toward income support.

The chapters that follow each contribute to our understanding of benefit issues in workers' compensation, an insurance program in a risky and uncertain world.

TABLE 1.1

Estimated Costs of Workers' Compensation to Employers, and Benefit Index, 1972–80

	Cost (in $ million)	Costs as a % of Payroll	Benefit Change Index
1972	$5,832	1.14%	100.0
1973	6,771	1.17	106.3
1974	7,881	1.24	112.6
1975	8,972	1.32	121.3
1976	11,045	1.49	129.3
1977	14,038	1.71	131.7
1978	17,000	1.86	136.7
1979	20,000	1.95	139.5
1980	22,000	1.96	143.3
1981	22,962	1.84	147.7
1982	22,529	1.72	154.1

Source: Price (1979, 1980, 1981, 1983). Figures for the benefit change index are from the National Council on Compensation Insurance.

2 · OCCUPATIONAL SAFETY AND HEALTH AND "IRRATIONAL" BEHAVIOR: A PRELIMINARY ANALYSIS

William T. Dickens

Few economists would argue that the perfect competition model of the labor market should be our primary guide in setting occupational safety and health (osh) policy. Nonetheless, little work has been done to elaborate alternative models for evaluating policy.[1] The lack of alternative models also makes it difficult to develop strong tests of the relevant predictions of the pure competition model. To develop strong tests, it is necessary to specify other models that have implications that are not consistent with the perfect competition model.[2] In the absence of knowledge of the ways, if any, in which the perfect competition model is inadequate, our policy discussions are even less well informed. The analysis that follows examines the effects of different policies when workers do not make the best possible decisions given the information available to them. Although the preliminary character of the analysis does not allow specific policy conclusions to be drawn,

I would like to thank Paula Mizelle for research assistance and the Institute of Industrial Relations for research support.

1. This is the conclusion of a recent survey of the literature on the theory of occupational safety and health regulation (Dickens 1984a).

2. An example of this approach is Viscusi (1979a and 1979c, 1980b), who does this with his model of adaptive worker behavior. Unfortunately he does not analyze market equilibrium in his model or the effects of osh policy.

the results point in a substantially new direction from past work on OSH regulation.

This chapter proceeds in four parts. First, I will define the type of behavior with which we will be concerned and provide a brief discussion of the reasons why people may be "irrational." After that, I will analyze the decisions workers make in taking a job and survey the evidence from psychological and behavioral decision theory research on the problems people are likely to have in making such decisions. Next, I will present a very simple model where workers are prone to one type of judgment error discussed in the second section. The model illustrates how consideration of such problems can complicate the analysis of OSH issues. For instance, it is shown that large compensating wage differentials are compatible with market failure, but these differentials need not reflect workers' valuations of their health or safety. The model is also shown to be consistent with the observed correlation between safety and turnover, the differences between injury rates for younger and older workers, and the differences between compensating wage differentials in the union and non-union sector. The potential role of OSH policy is also briefly considered. In the conclusion, I will discuss implications of the analysis for future work.

What do we mean when we say someone is irrational? I rely on the definition that appears to be most commonly used in economics—people are irrational if they do not make the best decisions possible given the information available to them.[3] Of course, it is not always possible to define the "best" decision in a particular situation. For this reason it is not always possible to define rational behavior.[4] I will proceed on the assumption that the problem of choosing the best job with respect to wages and safety is well defined, and that the choice process described by standard economic models is the best a worker can do.

Psychologists describe two broad reasons for irrational behav-

---

3. "Best possible" does not allow for cognitive limitations. Conceivably one could develop an economic theory of how people deal with cognitive limitations by making calculation and memory scarce resources. Other definitions of rationality have been proposed—for example, that choices should be consistent with the axioms of expected utility theory. This more limited view of rationality is not appropriate to the process being examined.
4. This is one of the primary criticisms of behavioral decision theory. See Einhorn and Hogarth (1981) for a review of the literature on this question.

ior. The first is motivation conflict; the second, limitations on cognitive capacity. Motivation conflict is thought to be the proximate cause of most mental illness. Since this kind of abnormal behavior is not of particular concern in most market situations and because it is relatively infrequent, it is not very important to most economic analysis. However, one type of behavior from this broad class has been singled out for attention by economists, namely, *cognitive dissonance*. Cognitive dissonance is said to exist when a person's past actions are inconsistent with some belief—usually a belief about one's own worth. Dissonant states are often resolved by the adjustment of other beliefs. The new beliefs may influence future behavior. Hirschman (1965) used cognitive dissonance to help describe attitudes towards change in the process of development. Akerlof and Dickens (1982) suggest a number of applications to economics, including choice of safety equipment when workers are subject to cognitive dissonance reactions.

Up until about fifteen years ago, most psychologists and economists were of the opinion that cognitive limitations were not a serious problem in most of our day-to-day activities. However, this view has begun to change. Slovic, Fischhoff, and Lichtenstein (1977) remark on the change in the psychological literature. More recently a number of economists have begun to take seriously the notion that cognitive limitations may influence economic behavior.[5]

The current interest in this phenomenon began with the observation that people who face problems dealing with probabilities, in the laboratory, violate many of the rules of expected utility maximization. After a number of these systematic departures from rational behavior were identified, an explanation for them was proposed. It has been hypothesized that most real world problems are far too complex for people to analyze on a case-by-case basis. As a result, humans have developed a set of decision-making strategies that work well in the most common situations. However, in some situations the strategies are not effective. Nonetheless, people persist in using them. In these instances we observe systematic deviations from rationality.

5. Grether and Plott (1979) consider the laboratory evidence for such problems. Kahneman and Tversky (1979) present a sketch of a theory of behavior that incorporates the laboratory evidence. Kunreuther (1978) applies the insights of psychological decision theory to a study of the purchase of disaster insurance. Arrow (1981) uses some of the same results to explain anomalies in the behavior of securities markets. Of course, Simon (for example, 1955) and Katona (1951) have long held such considerations to be important.

What are these situations? A more detailed review with reference to osh problems will follow. For now, suffice it to say that people seem to have difficulty dealing with choice problems that involve probabilistic events. The difficulty may be less severe when decisions are made by groups. In a group there is a greater likelihood that someone will propose the rational decision rule for a problem. This will usually ensure that a good decision is made, since it appears that people can recognize superior methods when they are proposed (Nisbett and Ross 1980, 266–67). In addition, there is some evidence that people may make better decisions when the stakes are higher. However, Grether and Plott (1979) find a slightly higher incidence of irrational behavior among subjects whose compensation for taking part in the experiment depends on their performance. Similarly, Borgida and Nisbett (1977) find that students making judgments about courses that they may take are more likely to make a certain judgment error than students who were less likely to take the courses. Finally, Slovic, Fischhoff, and Lichtenstein (1976) find that overconfidence about probabilistic judgments persists despite substantial incentives for realistic judgment. One hopeful note is that if a task is repeated several times, people's decisions may improve (Nisbett and Ross 1980, 291).

The decisions workers make about osh involve low-probability events, and are most often made by individuals and without much chance for repetition. Consequently, there is at least a prima facie case for giving further consideration to the sorts of problems people may have with such decisions.

The Workers' Decision-making Process: Potential Sources of Error

This section presents the workers' decision-making problem in choosing a job when osh is a consideration. Since employers' decisions are generally made by groups we will ignore them for now, although a similar analysis may well apply for small employers.

The workers' decision can be broken down into five steps. First, workers must gather information on available jobs. Once they have that information, they must assess the expected utility of each opportunity. Then, they must determine the value of additional information search. If the value exceeds the cost, they will gather more information repeating these three steps until the cost of the information search exceeds the expected value of the information. Once a worker has gathered enough information the worker will choose the job judged to provide the highest expected utility. While on the job, the worker must also decide how much effort to devote to self-protection and how much insurance to buy. Occasionally, a worker will receive new information about the nature of his or her job and other jobs. With new information a worker may consider changing jobs.

These five steps are represented in figure 2.1. At each stage in the decision-making process, people are liable to systematic judgment errors. What follows is an examination of the problems that have been identified by behavioral and psychological decision theory researchers which might affect judgments at each stage. One qualification is in order. Except where noted, judgment errors are not universal. Different people in similar situations may not behave the same. In addition, some tendencies may appear contradictory. In these cases both types of behavior are possible in different people in similar circumstances. One of the problems of predicting behavior is that people do not always apply the same strategies in what might appear to others

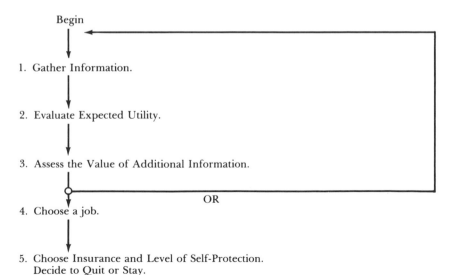

Figure 2.1
Schematic of a Worker's Decision-Making Process.

to be similar situations. Sometimes this will lead one person to do the opposite of another.

Information Gathering   Before people can decide to gather information on any aspect of employment, they must recognize the salience of that aspect to their decisions. Standard models of decision making assume people are aware of all salient features of a decision problem, but many real world decision-making problems have a far larger number of aspects than any person could reasonably be expected to consider. This would not be a serious problem if we could be sure that the strategies people used to decide which aspects to include in their analysis ensured that, in some sense, the most important were considered. Can we count on this happening? The answer, based on field studies of people's decisions about purchasing disaster insurance, seems to be no.

Kunreuther (1978) has argued that problem recognition is one of the most important barriers to people making rational decisions about disaster insurance. He found that over 40 percent of the residents of seismologically active areas believed that there was "no earthquake problem" where they live. Almost 75 percent of the people in floodplains did not consider floods to be a problem. If people making employment decisions do not consider job hazards to be a problem deserving consideration, they will not actively gather information on job safety and may be less inclined to remember such information if they happen upon it in examining other aspects of a job.

Another problem that is likely to interfere with information gathering is the tendency of preconceptions to interfere with observation. Any preconception about the nature of a phenomenon is likely to seriously affect a person's perception of that phenomenon. For instance, if we are told before meeting someone that the person is very bright, we will have a tendency to interpret the person's behavior as being indicative of intelligence (see Nisbett and Ross 1980, 93–101 and 168–75). To a certain extent, such interpretation of evidence does not create a problem. In many situations what people do may be a shorthand for more complicated and normatively correct filtering of information. But, there is substantial evidence that people are overly conservative in changing preconceptions in the face of new evidence.[6]

6. This was one of the early findings of psychological decision theory research. Slovic, Fischhoff, and Lichtenstein (1977) discuss this.

In fact, it has been found that any starting estimate of the nature of a phenomenon, even one that a subject knows to be completely arbitrary, will affect judgment (Tversky and Kahneman 1974). Certainly such behavior goes beyond what is normatively appropriate. Thus, if people enter the market with preconceptions about the safety of jobs, their assessments, after they have been exposed to new information, may change less than they should.

There is also evidence that people do not pay much attention to the quality of information. There is evidence that people pay no attention to sample size when gathering information (Nisbett and Ross 1980, 77–82 and 256–60; Slovic, Fischhoff, and Lichtenstein 1977). Further, it has been found that even totally nondiagnostic information may affect judgment (Nisbett, Zukier, and Lemley 1981). Such behavior may add more noise to workers' decisions. Finally, people may not discount evidence from biased samples even if they are aware of the bias (Nisbett and Ross 1980, 82–89 and 260–61). In most situations this is probably not important since the population one wishes to make inferences about is familiar. However, workers who hunt for information about a job by talking to workers who are still on that job may not consider the biased nature of the sample and discount the information received appropriately. Workers currently holding a job may see it in a better light than others who have considered the job and not taken it, or those who have quit. Similarly, a job seeker who talks to a worker who has quit may not recognize that this person's opinion of the job's quality may be biased downward.

Evaluating Expected Utility   In order to assess the expected utility from taking a job, a worker must first assess the probability distribution of the possible outcomes—how likely it is that he or she will be injured, killed, stay with the job for a certain number of years, and so on. Then the worker must assess the utility of each outcome and combine this with the assessment of the probability distribution of the possible outcomes to arrive at the expected utility of each job.

One of the most fundamental problems with human judgment about the likelihood of different outcomes is that it is inconsistent. People show a marked tendency to be inconsistent when repeating a judgment task unless they know they have done the task before and can remember their answer. The extent of this problem is illustrated by studies that have shown that, in many situations, simple rules derived from an expert decision maker's behavior performed better than the decision maker (Nisbett and Ross 1980, 140–41). A decision maker would be expected to do at least as well as a simple rule just by applying the rule. It is natural to assume that a human decision maker could outperform a rule by taking more factors into account. But, this is evidently not the case. It appears that human decision makers are either inconsistent in applying their own rules or are overly influenced by unique information not covered by the rules. Thus, even if workers have sufficient information to form accurate judgments of job hazards, their assessments may be subject to random judgment errors. If they are dealing with less than perfect information, their judgments will contain more error than would be caused by sampling differences alone.

Another almost universal problem is overconfidence. When people are asked to say how sure they are of a judgment they have made, they almost always report being more confident than is warranted given the available data. When people are asked to estimate confidence intervals on their judgments in real world situations, they consistently report intervals that prove to be too tight in light of subsequent events.[7] This type of error may result from people using simple models of complex phenomena and then not taking the possibility of specification error into account when projecting the likelihood of events. Such an error may lead workers to overestimate or underestimate the probability of a specific outcome. For instance, if a worker judges a job to be very safe, overconfidence about the judgment would cause the worker to discount the possibility that the job was less safe. The opposite could be true if the worker judged the job to be very unsafe.

In addition to these two very general problems with people's judgment, there are several others that apply to specific situations which are relevant to OSH decisions. First, it has been noted that vivid anecdotal information seems to have more of an impact on most people's judgment than more diagnostic statistical information.[8] Such

---

7. Slovic, Fischhoff, and Lichtenstein (1977), Einhorn and Hogarth (1981), and Nisbett and Ross (1980) all contain extensive discussions of the evidence for this problem.

8. This problem is also extensively discussed in Slovic, Fischhoff, and Lichtenstein (1977), Einhorn and Hogarth (1981), and Nisbett and Ross (1980, 18–24 and several other places throughout their book; see *vividness* and *availability heuristic* in their index).

information seems to be more easily recalled from memory. To determine how likely an event is, most people seem to try to see how easy it is to recall an incident of that event. Kahneman and Tversky (1979) have labeled this method of judging probability the "availability heuristic." This process is often functional. However, the inefficient use of information will contribute to inconsistency in judgment. To the extent that vivid accounts of accidents are more easily remembered than good safety records, there will be a tendency for people to overestimate the probability of accidents.[9]

Besides paying too much attention to vivid anecdotal information, people also have a demonstrable tendency to ignore base rate data in forming expectations (Nisbett and Ross 1980, 25–28 and 141–50). People will take extreme outcomes as being fully representative of the behavior of a process, even if they know that such behavior is unusual for similar processes (base rate information). For example, this may lead people to attribute too much importance to the accident experience of a particular firm, relative to the experience of other plants in the industry, in judging the safety of that plant.

Another form of judgment error is the tendency to attribute more control over a particular event to the people involved than they see themselves as having. This tendency is so pervasive that Ross (1977) dubbed it "the fundamental attribution error." People also have a tendency to interpret events as having a single cause (Nisbett and Ross 1980, 120–30). Together, these two tendencies may lead individuals to see accidents as being primarily the fault of the person who has the accident, rather than being, at least in part, a result of the working conditions at a plant.

Judgments about particular dangers are further complicated by the difficulty people have in discerning the existence of a relation between two phenomena when the correlation between them is small (Jennings, Amabile, and Ross 1980). This may cause people to fail to identify certain situations where there are low, but nontrivial, probabilities of an accident.

Another problem that has been identified is that many people

---

9. Another problem raised by this tendency is how to communicate information about work hazards. OSHA has tried to make its informational material more vivid and thus easier to recall. However, this has led employers to complain about the "inflammatory" style of presentation. Were OSHA to stick to neutral presentation of statistics the information might be less effectively conveyed.

seem not to comprehend basic concepts of probability. For instance, people behave as if they did not understand the meaning of independent events. When a low-probability event occurs people often behave as if they thought that it was less likely to happen again in the immediate future (Kunreuther 1978, 180). People also seem to behave as if they felt that the probabilities of extreme changes in their situation are less likely than objective information would indicate.[10] The familiar enunciation of this view is "it can't happen to me." Both of these lines of thinking may lead people to underestimate the danger of jobs. In the first case, people may think that because a place has had a serious accident in the immediate past it may be less likely to have another in the immediate future. In the second case, people may be willing to take dangerous jobs because they believe that they are unlikely to suffer an undesirable outcome.

People also have trouble judging the likelihood of compound events. If people are given the probability of event A and of event B and asked to judge the likelihood of A and B both occurring, they are likely to judge the probability as being between the probability of A and B rather than less than both of them (Kahneman and Tversky 1982). Such judgment errors may lead workers to overestimate the probability of accidents involving compound causes.

In addition to these potential problems in evaluating the nature of the probability distribution of possible outcomes, there are two major problems people can be expected to have in evaluating expected utility given the probability distribution. First, as I have mentioned, people may not recognize the relevance of OSH to the choice of employment. Second, people do not know what utility they will derive from a situation before they experience it. Instead, they must guess on the basis of past experience with similar situations or by doing thought experiments. Judgments about oneself are subject to much the same sorts of errors as judgments about the outside world.[11] Thus assessments of utility in different states of the world are likely to be biased and subject to inconsistency.

---

10. Kunreuther (1978) remarks about this tendency. Weber (1982) describes a theory of weighted utility that explains a number of anomalies in choice theory by assuming that people view large changes as less likely than objective probability indicates.

11. Nisbett and Ross (1980) devote all of chapters 9 and 10 to a review of the evidence on these questions.

Assessing the Value of Additional Information   Once people have determined the expected utility of the available jobs, they must decide whether they are ready to make a final decision or whether they need more information. If they are rational economic decision makers, they will weigh the value of additional information against the cost of acquiring it. The value of information depends on, among other things, how certain one is of one's estimates of the state of the world. Someone who is very sure about his or her estimate will see little value to additional information. Someone who is less sure will see information as being more valuable. As was noted earlier, people are almost always overconfident about their judgments. Thus they will probably have a tendency to collect too little information.[12]

Choosing a Job   If people behaved in the way described by standard economic theory, once they evaluated the utility of each job they would choose the job that promised the highest expected utility. However, people do not seem to make decisions that way.

　　People often do not use all the information available to them. Kahneman and Tversky (1979) propose a theory of behavior based on their interpretation of laboratory evidence of how people make decisions when confronted with probabilistic outcomes. According to the theory, people edit out certain information in choosing among lotteries. When given a choice among several options, people tend to decide by doing comparisons of pairs of options, discarding the one that is least preferred and comparing the most preferred one to the next option. In comparing two options, not all information is considered. People will not concern themselves with a particular trait if the two options being considered are similar with respect to that trait. Low-probability outcomes may also be ignored.

　　Because of these and other editing rules, a person's choice may depend on the sequence in which options are considered. Which editing rules an individual applies depend on the nature of the options and other factors that are unique to the individual and the situation. Also, some people may not pay any attention to injury probabilities if these are sufficiently small—even if the expected loss in the event

---

12. The problem of information search has been investigated in the behavioral decision theory literature without reference to overconfidence. See Connolly and Gilani (1982).

of injury is high. This is illustrated by laboratory studies of people's behavior in purchasing disaster insurance.

Kunreuther (1978) conducted some laboratory experiments in which subjects played a farm management game. Several times in the course of the game subjects were offered the option of purchasing actuarially fair insurance against hazards that ranged in probability from .002 to .250, and all had the same expected cost (probability × loss). On average, people in this experiment were much more likely to purchase insurance against the more probable but less costly hazards than against the very costly improbable hazards. When subjects were questioned about their decisions, most indicated that they had not considered the event likely enough to warrant further thought (Kunreuther 1978, 183), even though the cost of such events was relatively high.

Choosing Insurance, Self-Protection Measures, and Deciding to Change Jobs   All the problems previously described will also be relevant to these decisions. In addition, there will be two more problems. First, one now has a strong theory—that one's job is the best job—which will interfere with interpretation of new evidence. As was noted earlier, people tend to interpret data as being consistent with any theory they hold to be true, and to disregard information which contradicts the theory. Second, once someone has chosen a job, cognitive dissonance phenomena, as described by Akerlof and Dickens (1982), become relevant.[13] Both of these tendencies will lead people to see their jobs as safer than they actually are.

What can we conclude, from this review, about the nature of individual decisions? The first important concepts that can be abstracted from this list include problem recognition and information editing. Several authors have suggested that people may not always be aware of or pay attention to low-probability outcomes in choosing between alternatives. Thus some workers may pay no attention to OSH when choosing jobs.

The second general problem is that judgments will be inac-

---

13. Bem (1967) has suggested that cognitive dissonance phenomena may not result from motivational conflict but rather from errors in self-attribution—people may not know why they do some things and may generate an explanation by assuming they believed something other than what they did. Although this is not consistent with the normative interpretation suggested by Akerlof and Dickens (1982), it still leads to the same implications for behavior.

curate and inconsistent for a host of reasons. In addition, there are several sources of potential bias working in both directions; thus it is impossible to say a priori whether people will behave as if they thought jobs were more or less safe than they actually are. Finally, once workers are on the job, there will probably be a tendency for them to view their jobs as being safer than they actually are.

The Market for OSH in the Presence of Irrational Behavior

Before attempting to develop a model that integrates all three of these major tendencies, it is useful to consider simpler models that abstract only one major observation from the list of problems just described. Such an approach allows us to identify which types of behavior yield important results so that the behavior may be studied in greater detail. They also allow us to anticipate what type of behavior is likely from more complicated and realistic models.

Akerlof and Dickens (1982) consider a model where workers' decisions to take a job may affect later assessments of the job's safety. Despite the assumption that workers are aware of the potential for such effects, there may still be a role for OSH policy. The model is highly stylized and as such yields few empirical predictions. The one implication of such a model—that workers in a job will view it as safer than others who have not taken the job—also obtains in another type of model.

If workers, because of imperfect information or judgment errors, had different assessments of a job's utility (as with the second major type of problem discussed earlier), then the workers in a job would tend to be those who see it as safer than it actually is. A model with these properties has been considered by Perloff and Salop (1980) and Dickens (1984a). Perloff and Salop show that firms in such a market will have monopsony power. Dickens considers the incentives for employers to provide safety in such a model and the effects of OSH policy. Dickens shows that even if the average worker believes all jobs are safer than they are, employers may still provide an efficient amount of safety; but that even it they do, safety standards may improve welfare by eliminating monopsony power.

What has not been considered is how markets will behave if some workers pay no attention to safety while others do. Following is an exploration of some simple models where this assumption is made about worker behavior.

It will be assumed that workers will choose jobs to maximize subjective expected utility. For this analysis, the safety of a job will be described in terms of the probability of an accident. People's true expected utility will depend on the wage they are paid and on the safety of the job. However, it will be assumed that the probability of an accident, even in the worst case, will be small enough that some workers will not recognize the probability as relevant in comparing jobs. These workers will behave as if their expected utility did not depend on safety. These workers will be referred to as being *nonattentive* to safety. Workers who do use the information will be referred to as *attentive*. It will be assumed that the number of each type of worker is fixed.

Workers will find jobs in a market of perfectly competitive firms. For now we will assume that all the firms produce the same product and have the same U-shaped long-run average cost curves and the same cost per worker of providing safety given the level of safety chosen. The market demand curve for the firms' product will be downward sloping. A firm's profit function, given the number of other firms in the industry, can be written as

$$\pi = R(L) - Lc(p) - Lw, \tag{2.1}$$

where π is the firm's profit, R is the revenue as a function of the amount of labor hired (L), and $c(p)$ is the cost per worker of providing safety. The probability of an accident is p, and w is the wage. First-order conditions for profit maximization yield

$$R' = c(p) + w. \tag{2.2}$$

Workers' wages plus the cost of safety must equal the workers' marginal revenue product. With pure competition in the product market, $MRP = VMP$. To ensure the existence of an equilibrium, we will also assume the existence of a p^* such that $c'(p^*) = c(p^*) = 0$ and that $c' < 0$ for $p < p^*$ and $c'' > 0$.

What will equilibrium in such a market look like? I will describe an equilibrium and then explain why it is the only possible equilibrium consistent with these assumptions. First, firms will specialize in one of two categories—either they will employ attentive workers or nonattentive workers. In competitive equilibrium, all firms must be producing at the least average cost, so they must all employ the same amount of labor and have the same marginal cost of labor. Thus $w + c(p)$ must be the same for all firms. The number of firms will be determined by the number of workers. The number of workers will also determine the amount that is produced, the price, and thus the $VMP(R')$. Firms employing nonattentive workers will choose $p = p^*$ and offer a wage equal to $w_n = R'$. Firms hiring attentive workers will choose p such that

$$c'(p) = \frac{\dfrac{d\text{SEU}}{dp}}{\dfrac{d\text{SEU}}{dw}}, \tag{2.3}$$

where SEU is the subjective expected utility of the attentive workers. They will then offer a wage of

$$w_c = R' - c(p_c) < w_n. \tag{2.4}$$

It should be clear that it is impossible for a firm to enter this market offering any combination of wages and safety besides these two and still earn positive profits. Thus there cannot be more than two types of firms. Unless $p^* = p_c$, it will also be impossible for equilibrium to exist with less than two types of firms. If there is only one wage and safety pair offered, it is possible for other firms to enter and earn positive profits. Thus the only possible competitive equilibrium is the one described above with two types of firms.

What should be noted about this equilibrium? First, workers in the more hazardous jobs receive higher wages even though they are not aware of the dangers facing them. It is a property of this model, and several other similar models (Dickens 1984a), that competition will create compensating wage differentials, even if all workers are not aware of the hazards they face. However, these wage differentials have nothing to do with how workers perceive the costs of an accident. Rather, a hedonic wage equation estimated from data on a market like this would measure only the firm's cost curve—not the worker's marginal rate of substitution of safety and wages in utility (MRS), as is commonly assumed. If the production technology is convex in safety, as has been assumed above, and the MRS in labor demand for the attentive workers is equal to the MRS in utility,[14] then the

---

14. This will be true if attentive workers are completely rational and may still be true if workers make judgment errors about the level of safety, as long as they correctly perceive marginal changes in that level in terms of expected utility.

estimated slope of the hedonic wage equation is necessarily less than the MRS of the attentive workers. This can be seen in figure 2.2. Thus the "value of life" estimated from hedonic wage studies will tend to underestimate people's true preferences.

The second thing to note is that the workers who have not paid any attention to safety in their decisions could be made better off if the probability of accidents on their jobs was lowered. Thus there is a potential role for policy to play. Oi (1973) and Chelius (1977) both discount the possibility that judgment errors could lead to an under-provision of safety, because it is the perceptions of the marginal worker in a firm—who most likely has the least favorable view of the firm's safety—whose judgments count in the firm's decisions. While this may be true for each firm, if the market is big enough to allow segmentation, then underprovision is possible and there may be a role for policy. This is the case in the model presented here.

What if we relax the assumption that firms all face the same costs? Will these results still hold? To analyze this question, let us look at a model like the one just described, except that in this new model there are firms from two different industries. Each industry faces a downward sloping demand curve for its product. We will assume that the safety level in one industry is fixed and that the probability of an accident (p_s) is very low. We will refer to this as the safe industry. The

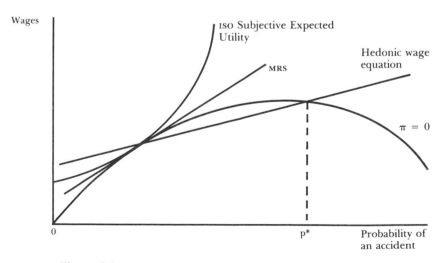

Figure 2.2
Relation of Hedonic Wage Equation to MRS in Utility.

probability of an accident in the other industry depends on the safety expenditures of the firms in that industry. We will also assume that the cost of reducing the probability of an accident in the "unsafe" industry is sufficiently high that if marginal products are equal in the two industries, attentive workers will prefer the wage safety pair (R', p_s) to any that could be offered by the unsafe industry.

Competition will guarantee that if nonattentive workers are employed in both industries, their wages will be equal. If attentive workers are employed in both industries, their subjective expected utility will be equal.

The character of equilibrium in this world will depend on the demand conditions in the two industries and on the number of workers of each type. We will analyze the types of equilibrium that may result by holding the total number of workers and demand conditions constant, and varying the percentage of workers who pay attention to safety.

If all workers ignore safety in choosing their jobs, then the unsafe industry will choose safety so that $c'(p) = c(p) = 0$ and will set the wage equal to the marginal product of labor. Since there are no costs to providing safety level p_S in the safe industry, labor will allocate itself between the two industries so that

$$R'_s = R'_u = w_u^n = w_s^n \tag{2.5}$$

where R' is the marginal product of labor, w is the wage, the subscripts s and u refer to the safe and unsafe industry, and the superscripts indicate that the wages are being paid to workers who are not attentive to safety.

If some of the nonattentive workers now begin to pay attention to the safety of their jobs, they will choose employment in the safe industry. They will do this because the wages in the two are equal and the safety is greater in the safe industry. Because we have assumed that $c(p_s)$ is prohibitively high, and since $R'_s = R'_u$, it will be impossible for employers in the unsafe industry to attract attentive workers. If some of the newly attentive workers come from the unsafe industry they will temporarily lower the marginal product of labor in the safe industry. This will displace an equal number of nonattentive workers who will move into the unsafe industry. After the adjustment, wages and marginal products in both industries will be the same as the case when all workers were nonattentive.

If we continue to increase the percentage of workers who are attentive to safety, this process of displacement will continue until all nonattentive workers have left the safe industry. If we continue to increase the percentage of attentive workers beyond this point, the marginal product and the wage of labor in the unsafe industry will begin to rise, and the marginal product and the wage of labor in the safe industry will fall. This will continue until the marginal product of labor in the unsafe industry becomes sufficiently high so as to allow employers in that industry to pay a compensating wage differential that will attract workers from the safe industry. At this point they will begin to offer jobs with a safety level such that the condition described by equation 2.3 is satisfied and to offer a wage in that job equal to

$$R'_u - c(p_u^a) = w_u^a < w_u^n. \tag{2.6}$$

Such jobs may either be safer or less safe than jobs in the safe industry. If they are safer, they will pay less than the jobs in the safe industry since competition requires that the subjective expected utility of the two jobs be equal.

Thus as long as nonattentive workers are not employed in the safe industry, compensating wage differentials will be paid. In this case the differentials depend not only on the costs of providing safety but also on market conditions and the costs of production. In all cases nonattentive workers would benefit from regulations that improved job safety.

Although this is a very simple and highly stylized model, it is still interesting to see if it is consistent with what we know about the market provision of OSH. We turn now to that task. First, as has already been noted, this theory is entirely consistent with observed compensating wage differences paid to workers in dangerous jobs. Beyond this, there are several other findings that can be considered. Viscusi (1979a and 1979c) observes that worker quit rates are positively correlated with unsafe working conditions. He shows that this result could be expected if workers were behaving like Bayesian decision makers who had imperfect information about job safety. However, this observation may also be consistent with the type of model discussed here. If we were to assume that nonattentive workers who became attentive would quit their jobs to look for a safer job and that some proportion of workers who experience an accident will become attentive,[15] then we would observe no turnover among attentive workers (who are in the safer jobs) and turnover rates among nonattentive workers proportional to the probability of injury on their jobs.

Once we allow experience to affect workers' attentiveness to safety, the model also becomes consistent with the observation that younger workers tend to experience a greater number of accidents (Dillingham 1981 and Chelius 1979). This fact has normally been attributed to the inexperience of younger workers, which makes them more accident prone than older workers. But, younger workers are also more agile and have more acute senses, so the explanation is not completely convincing. On the other hand, if young workers are more likely to be nonattentive because of their lack of experience, then they would be more likely to be in dangerous jobs and would have a higher incidence of injuries.

It has also been shown that compensating wage differences for exposure to potentially fatal hazards are much larger for union than for nonunion workers. Viscusi (1980c) attempts to explain these results by arguing that the unions' objective is to maximize the total surplus of all workers. Thus the compensating differentials should reflect the preferences of what Viscusi calls an average worker. He notes that in nonunion firms the compensating wage differential will reflect the preferences of only the marginal worker. Viscusi argues that younger workers are more likely to be marginal and will have less interest in safety than other workers, and thus union members should receive larger compensating differences. However, if differences in tastes are that large, there are very strong incentives for employers and workers to agree to mutually advantageous market segmentation. Inframarginal workers could offer to trade wage reductions for safety. This would result in wage premiums commensurate with tastes for all workers. Thus it is unlikely that Viscusi's explanation will suffice.[16]

---

15. Kunreuther (1978, 156–59) notes that personal experiences with a hazard is a prime determinant of problem recognition.

16. Viscusi (1980c) argues that they have no incentive to do this because by revealing their preferences they allow the firm to capture the entire surplus. However, this need not be the case. Workers could reveal their marginal preferences and engage in mutually advantageous trade with their employers without revealing the size of their surplus.

Olson suggests that unions may provide more information to their workers about the hazards they face and thus cause them to demand larger differentials. However, except in the extreme case where workers assume that the probability of an accident is zero, it is not clear that giving them more information will cause wage differentials to increase (Dickens 1984a). Also, if information differences lead to such large changes in compensating differentials, then the value of information must be very high, which makes it hard to understand why workers would not engage more in information search.

While existing theory does not provide a good explanation for these results, they do fit very neatly into the judgment error model just described. Recall that one factor which substantially improved judgment was group decision making. In the extreme we might expect only union decision makers to be attentive and all other workers to be nonattentive. If this were the case we would find compensating differentials between union and nonunion workers and within the subset of union workers, but not within the subset of nonunion workers. This is what a review of the literature on union-nonunion differences reveals (Dickens 1984b).

The one observation which is difficult to reconcile with this model is that over half of all blue-collar workers report that their jobs expose them to some danger. In addition, this self-reported danger is positively related to wages after controlling for other factors (Viscusi 1979a). If we were to interpret people's reporting that they are exposed to danger as indicating that they were attentive to safety, then we would expect that self-reported danger would be negatively correlated with wages after controlling for other factors. If we were to interpret self-reported danger as being indicative of both attentiveness and above average danger, we would have to conclude that nearly all workers were attentive. However, it is not clear that either of these interpretations are appropriate. Workers who report that their job exposes them to some danger may not have considered the danger when taking their current job and may not consider it relevant to any future decision to change jobs. The meaning of the question is further complicated because what people mean by danger may differ. Some who report not being exposed to danger mean that they are not exposed to extreme danger. Others who report being exposed may refer to trivial hazards. Finally, when the effect of this self-report variable on earnings is broken down according to union and nonunion sectors, it has a significant effect only in the union sector and only in a linear specification (Viscusi 1979c). In the nonunion sector and in the union sector, when the log of earnings is the dependent variable, the standard error is larger than the coefficient. Thus it is not clear how to interpret this finding, and it should not be interpreted as proof that a lack of attentiveness to safety is not a problem.

Conclusion

I hope this paper has convinced readers that more attention should be paid to questions of the rationality of workers in dealing with osh. The evidence from psychological decision theory research strongly suggests that people do not behave the way they are assumed to in standard economic analysis. The laboratory evidence is backed up by field studies and observations of people's behavior in a number of real world situations—some very similar to the problems encountered by workers making osh decisions. These studies suggest that the laboratory evidence is relevant to real world problems.

In addition, the simple, stylized model was found to be consistent with almost all of what we know about the provision of osh in labor markets. With respect to the evidence on the compensating differences paid union as opposed to nonunion workers, the model provides a better explanation than does the existing literature.

Taken together, this evidence strongly suggests that a model based on the behavioral theory is preferable to the standard economic model for evaluating the welfare impact of different regulatory programs. The two models developed in previous work and the one presented in this chapter all allow a beneficial role for policy intervention. Further consideration of behavioral models may shed light on the efficacy of different programs for improving osh. Should we give workers additional information or fine employers with bad safety records? Should existing engineering standards be extended?

If further research is pursued, what form should it take? A first step would be to work out the implications of the rest of the problems I have discussed. Such an enterprise may suggest some tests of the importance of these types of behavior for osh decisions. Thus the theoretical work may motivate a program of empirical work. The ultimate goal of such a program would be to identify which behavioral considerations are most important for modeling OSH decisions.

It also seems likely that even if people were fully rational, there would still be problems with imperfect information in markets for OSH. Since many of the decision-making problems I have discussed involve information perception and processing, it would probably be useful to integrate models of these phenomena with models of the behavior of markets with imperfect information.

3 · THE COSTS AND BENEFITS OF OSHA-INDUCED INVESTMENTS IN EMPLOYEE SAFETY AND HEALTH

Ann P. Bartel and Lacy Glenn Thomas

The strategy for accident reduction embodied in the Occupational Safety and Health Act (OSHA) of 1970 is largely based on capital equipment standards. While these standards have the virtue of being easily monitored, critics have argued that they address only a small part of the complex epidemiology of accident causation and thus are likely to have minimal impact on injury rates. After a decade of experience with OSHA enforcement of these standards, an assessment of the costs and benefits of industrial investments in employee safety and health is in order. This assessment is particularly needed in light of the substantial magnitudes of industrial investments in employee safety and health; in some industries these investments have been in excess of 5 percent of total investment spending in a given year.[1]

  An important issue for any study of industrial safety investment is the extent to which OSHA is itself responsible for this investment and its resulting costs and benefits. Weidenbaum and de Fina (1978), in their widely cited study of the economywide costs of federal regulation, have argued that OSHA requirements accounted for 100 percent of all industrial safety investment. Unfortunately, this argument

---

1. Documented in the McGraw-Hill Company's *Annual Survey of Investment in Employee Safety and Health.*

amounted to unsubstantiated assumption. In his econometric investigation of this issue, Viscusi (1979b) found the diametrically opposite result—that OSHA enforcement had no effect whatsoever on industrial investment, a finding he attributed to the alleged weak relationship between OSHA enforcement efforts and industrial compliance.

There are two reasons for reexamining Viscusi's (1979b) findings. First, Viscusi used a rather disaggregate set of annual investment data (sixty industries) prepared by McGraw-Hill and Company. Subsequent to publication of Viscusi's article, McGraw-Hill ceased to publish new disaggregate data and withdrew the old disaggregate publications because of statistical weakness of the estimates. Further, McGraw-Hill has recently issued a revised historical series of more aggregate investment data (eighteen industries) covering the years from 1972 to 1979. A reexamination of OSHA's effect on safety investment using the corrected data seems to be in order.

Second, although it has been argued by Viscusi (1979b) and others that OSHA's enforcement effort is weak, our recent work (Bartel and Thomas 1985) on industrial compliance indicates that this argument has been severely overstated. Our results show that there are significant effects of OSHA enforcement on industry violation rates, although the link between noncompliance and workplace accidents is considerably weaker.

In light of these issues, it seems useful at this time to reexamine the impact of OSHA's efforts on industrial investment in employee safety and health. We first present a theoretical framework for estimating the determinants and consequences of this type of industrial investment. Next we describe the data sources and empirical specifications, address the limitations that are inherent in the available data, and point out potential biases in our results. We then present the results of estimating the model and conclude with implications for policy.

Theoretical Framework

The Production Function for Safety   The injury rate in a given industry at time period t is determined by the stock of safety capital per worker in that industry:

$$AE_t = f(K_t, \mathbf{H}_t), \tag{3.1}$$

where AE_t = accidents per worker at time t, K_t = the stock of safety capital per worker at time t, and $\mathbf{H_t}$ is a vector of hazardousness characteristics such as technology, characteristics of workers, and the pace of work.[2] A substantial literature on the role played by these variables exists and is best summarized in Oi's (1974) survey article. Briefly, the technological variables that have been found to be important in the production function for industrial safety are average firm size, percentage of production workers, percentage of unionized workers, and the labor to capital ratio.[3] Characteristics of the work force such as education and the rate of new hires have been found to be significant determinants of the injury rate, because less educated and less experienced workers tend to be accident prone. Finally, workplace injury rates are likely to be correlated with the amount of overtime work, since tired workers will be less careful in the operation of machinery.

Investments in Safety Capital   The industry's objective is to maximize profits, and the stock of safety capital is an important determinant of the profit level. On the one hand, a greater stock of safety capital per worker will result in fewer injuries, and thus industry profits will increase because of fewer lost or restricted workdays and smaller wage premiums to compensate for job-related risks. On the other hand, increasing the stock of safety capital may require costly investments that will reduce profits.

In the absence of OSHA enforcement, each industry will choose that level of safety capital that maximizes its profits. OSHA's enforcement activities are geared toward penalizing firms that have not achieved the prescribed safety standards. For example, if K^* is the per worker safety capital standard set by OSHA and K is the stock of safety capital per worker chosen by the industry, where $K < K^*$, then the industry will have to pay a penalty to OSHA. The industry then can find its optimal stock of safety capital per worker by maximizing the following expected profit function at any time t:

$$\pi_t = NET_t(K_t) - (IE)[P(K_t{}^* - K_t)], \tag{3.2}$$

where *NET* represents industry revenues minus *all* costs except those due to fines for violations of OSHA standards, *IE* is the probability of

---

2. The approach here is similar to that used by Viscusi (1979b).
3. In our own work we have also used the rate of worker complaints to OSHA as a proxy for the degree of hazard to which workers are exposed.

inspection by OSHA, and $P(K_t^* - K_t)$ is the penalty imposed if K_t^* exceeds K_t.

The profit-maximizing stock of safety capital per worker is given by:

$$NET_t'(K_t) - IE(P') = 0, \tag{3.3}$$

where $NET' < 0$ and $P' < 0$. We can use this equation to generate predictions about the determinants of the industry's optimal stock of safety capital.

According to equation (3.3), an increase in the intensity of OSHA enforcement, as measured by the probability of inspection, will induce the industry to choose a larger stock of safety capital per worker.

A primary determinant of NET, and hence the industry stock of safety capital, is the industry's marginal productivity of investing in such capital. This marginal productivity schedule will differ across industries because of differences in their production technologies. Two variables can be used as proxies for this marginal productivity schedule. First, the general profitability of investment in the industry is given by total capital investments per worker XE_t. Second, the specific profitability of investments in safety capital can be proxied by industry compliance with OSHA standards. High levels of *non-compliance* with these standards indicate lower marginal productivity of investment and lower optimal investment rates. We use last period's noncompliance rate (PI_{t-1}) to avoid simultaneity problems. We thus expect the following derivative restrictions:

$$INV_{XE_t} > 0 \qquad INV_{PI_{t-1}} < 0. \tag{3.4}$$

It is important to distinguish the concept of *natural noncompliance* from the concept of *natural hazardousness*, which measures the degree of unregulated worker safety. For example, police work is naturally compliant with OSHA regulations given the technology of the industry but is also naturally hazardous. Thus there is no expected relation between the accident rate and levels of safety investment when the components of the vector of natural noncompliance variables are properly modeled.

Whenever one firm suffers a greater cost burden per employee as regulations are evenly enforced across firms, a *compliance asymmetry* results. When these asymmetries exist, certain firms will suffer higher per employee compliance costs and thus will be competitively disadvantaged. There appear to be two principal sources of compliance asymmetries resulting from OSHA regulations. First, several scholars have documented the existence of economies of scale in compliance with regulation. When large firms experience these economies, their marginal productivity schedule for safety investment is higher, and they will find higher levels of safety investment to be profitable. Second, to the extent that unionized firms exhibit higher preregulation stocks of safety capital, their marginal productivity of investment is lower, and they will be observed to have lower investment rates. The implication of this is that OSHA enforcement causes nonunionized firms to suffer higher investment rates to avoid noncompliance penalties. Thus we expect the following derivative restrictions:

$$INV_{EF} > 0 \qquad INV_{UE} < 0. \tag{3.5}$$

The investment equation then is

$$INV_t = f(IE_t, XE_t, PI_{t-1}, EF_t, UE_t). \tag{3.6}$$

OSHA Enforcement Behavior   In our earlier study (Bartel and Thomas 1985) we developed a model of how OSHA allocates inspections among industries based on the economic theory of regulation.[4] This model emphasized the importance of "indirect effects" of regulation. Traditional analyses of regulation have long focused on what we call the "direct effects" of regulation—the isolated, partial equilibrium impacts on single firms or individuals. Among the direct effects of OSHA are improvements in safety for workers and increases in manufacturing costs that decrease profits and wages. Alongside these direct effects, however, are the more general equilibrium "indirect effects"—the competitive advantages that arise from the asymmetrical impacts of regulation among different groups of firms and workers. For example, if the cost burden of certain regulations falls heavily on one group of firms and lightly on a second group, then, an indirect effect of these regulations is to provide a competitive advantage to the second group of firms. It is extremely important to recognize that for many firms and workers the indirect effects of regulation can outweigh, in terms of economic importance, the direct effects.

Recognition of the importance of indirect effects shifts the

---

4. This theory was developed in Stigler (1971) and Peltzman (1976).

focus of analysis from safety cost-benefit issues within individual firms to political wealth transfer issues among heterogenous firms in inspected industries. Specifically, we found that OSHA concentrated enforcement efforts on smaller (in terms of number of employees) and nonunion firms. This more vigorous enforcement against small and nonunion firms placed a greater cost burden on them, putting them at a competitive disadvantage with respect to larger and more unionized competitors. It is important to recognize that these enforcement asymmetries are distinct from and can reinforce the compliance asymmetries discussed earlier with regard to the investment equation.

The enforcement equation estimated is

$$\log IE_t = \gamma_0 + \gamma_1 \mathbf{X_t} + \gamma_2 \log INV_t + \gamma_3 \log UE_t \qquad (3.7)$$
$$+ \gamma_4 \log EF_t + \gamma_5 (\log EF_t) \cdot t.$$

where $\mathbf{X_t}$ is a vector of additional variables as discussed in the following section. The sign of γ_2 is not predictable theoretically, as is discussed at length in our earlier paper (Bartel and Thomas 1985). The signs of γ_3 and γ_4 are negative, because of expected enforcement asymmetries. Finally, in our earlier study, we exposed the fact that, over time, OSHA shifted enforcement efforts away from small firms, in response to increasingly sophisticated pressure in Congress by small firms for relief from OSHA regulation. The sign of γ_5 on the firm size-time interaction term is thus positive.

Data and Empirical Specifications

Data Sources   The only source of data on industrial investment in employee safety and health is the McGraw-Hill *Annual Survey of Investment in Employee Safety and Health.* For the manufacturing sector (which is the focus of our analysis), McGraw-Hill collected data for eighteen two-digit industry categories.[5] The data are presented in two forms: dollar investment in employee safety and health, and employee safety and health investment as a percentage of capital spending.

Data on OSHA's enforcement activities were obtained from the agency for the time period 1972 through 1978. These data are restricted to firms located in the twenty-two states where safety regu-

---

5. The industry categories are: iron and steel, nonferrous metals, electrical machinery, machinery, autos, trucks and parts, aerospace, other transportation equipment, fabricated metals, instruments, stone, clay and glass, other durables, chemicals, paper, rubber, petroleum, food and beverages, textiles, and other nondurables.

lations have been directly enforced by OSHA during the entire 1972–78 period.[6] Under provisions of OSHA of 1970, states may retain responsibility for development and enforcement of OSHA standards. State standards must be "at least as effective" as national standards, and adequate personnel must be assigned to enforcement. OSHA must delegate the authority to those states that submit an acceptable program to the Secretary of Labor, whereupon the Department of Labor may reimburse up to 50 percent of those states' administrative and enforcement costs. Unfortunately, there are substantial differences in the relative vigor of federal and state enforcement efforts. Data provided by OSHA (1979) indicate that each federal inspector visits 60 percent more workers than does each state inspector, that federal inspections are almost three times as likely to cite firms with serious violations as are state inspections, and that federal fines per violation *within* comparable classes of violation are almost twice the rate assessed at the state level. In light of these profound differences between federal and state jurisdictions, it is inappropriate to combine data on inspection activities in the twenty-two states under the federal program with the twenty-eight states under the state program. The data set from OSHA contains information for each three-digit manufacturing industry on the number of inspections and the dollar value of penalties.

Information on occupational injury rates was obtained from the Bureau of Labor Statistics. We have chosen to use the lost workdays rate (lost workdays per 100 full-time workers) as our measure of the industry's accident rate.

Data on the demographic and technological characteristics of the industries have been collected from several sources. First, from the *Employment and Earnings* files of the Bureau of Labor Statistics, we have information on percentages of production workers, percentages of male workers, average hourly earnings, average overtime hours, and the new hire rate. Second, from the *Current Population Survey*, we have data on percentages of unionized workers and average education of the employees. Third, we used the Bureau of the Census's *Annual Survey of Manufacturers* to obtain information on labor costs, value of

---

6. Those states are Alabama, Arkansas, Delaware, District of Columbia, Florida, Georgia, Idaho, Kansas, Louisiana, Maine, Massachusetts, Mississippi, Missouri, Nebraska, Ohio, New Hampshire, Oklahoma, Pennsylvania, Rhode Island, South Dakota, Texas, and West Virginia.

shipments, and value of assets and capital investment. Fourth, from the bureau's *County Business Patterns* tapes, we obtained data on the number and size distribution (by employees) of establishments for each three-digit Standard Industrial Classification (sic) for the twenty-two states under federal jurisdiction. Restricting our analysis to the twenty-two states was necessary in order to correctly estimate the industry's probability of inspection. In other words, since our inspection data referred to the twenty-two states only, the calculation of inspections per employee required that the denominator also be based on that sample. It should be noted that the disaggregated *County Business Patterns* data that are necessary for the twenty-two-state restriction are only available beginning with 1974. In addition, the coding of the data required that the number of employees in each industry and year had to be estimated using the following formula:

$$\text{Total number of workers} = \sum_{i=1}^{7} F_i M_i, \tag{3.8}$$

where F_i = number of establishments in size class i and M_i = average ratio of workers to establishments in size class i. For the largest size class (with more than a thousand workers in each establishment), we assumed that M_i equaled the average number of employees for national firms of comparable size in that industry. Note that M_i is constant across all industries except in the largest size class. The industry-varying national average firm size for the largest size class was obtained from the published volumes of *County Business Patterns*.

Empirical Specifications: Investment in Safety   An important consideration for our empirical analysis is that the McGraw-Hill data refer to only a sample of United States manufacturing firms, whereas the data that we use to measure the demographic and technological characteristics of the industries refer to all manufacturing firms. We attempt to correct for this by creating a safety investment variable that pertains to all United States manufacturing firms. The variable is defined as follows for each industry in our sample:

$$SAFEINV = \frac{\left(\begin{array}{l}\text{safety investment as a percent-}\\\text{age of capital spending in the}\\\text{McGraw-Hill sample}\end{array}\right)\left(\begin{array}{l}\text{capital spending in the}\\\text{\textit{Annual Survey of Manu-}}\\\text{\textit{facturers'} sample}\end{array}\right)}{\left(\begin{array}{l}\text{number of employees in}\\\text{the industry in the}\\\text{entire U.S.}\end{array}\right)\left(\text{price deflator}\right)}. \tag{3.9}$$

This variable is a proxy for safety investment per employee on a national basis. Hence, based on our previous discussion, we estimate the following safety investment equation:[7]

$$\ln(SAFEINV) = \alpha_0 + \alpha_1 \ln(INSP) + \alpha_2 \ln(CAPEXP) +$$
$$\alpha_3 \ln(PENLAG) + \alpha_4 \ln(FSIZE) + \quad (3.10)$$
$$\alpha_5 \ln(UNION) + \alpha_6 \ln(LDAY) +$$
$$\alpha_7 YRDUM + \mu_1,$$

where:
$INSP$ = number of OSHA inspections/number of employees;
$CAPEXP$ = total capital expenditures in the industry;
$PENLAG$ = penalties per inspection last year;
$FSIZE$ = average firm size in the industry (for the entire U.S.);
$UNION$ = percentage of employees who are unionized;
$LDAY$ = the lost workday rate; and
$YRDUM$ = a set of dummy variables for the various years.

We recognize that data limitations require us to interpret the results of estimating equation 3.10 with extreme caution. As previously explained, the inspection and penalty data refer to the twenty-two state region that has been continuously subject to federal enforcement, while the McGraw-Hill investment data are available only on a national level. Collection of historical enforcement data from twenty-nine separate state agencies, many of which did not have adequately funded data collection efforts, is a task beyond the scope of this study. Any study of OSHA's effect on industrial safety investment must thus compare national expenditure patterns with regional enforcement frequencies. If state agencies precisely duplicate within their jurisdictions the pattern of federal enforcement frequencies, then these comparisons are unbiased. To the extent that state agencies employ unique enforcement strategies however, the national OSHA enforcement effort is measured with error by the regional OSHA data. An additional problem with equation 3.10 is that the highly aggregative nature of the McGraw-Hill data may well obscure significant differences among industries.

---

7. The lost workday variable is included in this equation to control for a possible simultaneous relationship between accidents and safety investments. But recall from our earlier discussion that we do not expect to observe an effect of accidents on investment.

Empirical Specifications: The Effect of Safety Investments on the Injury Rate We can use equation 3.1 to show how investments in safety capital will affect the injury rate. First, we will specify this equation as follows:

$$AE_t = \exp(-\alpha K_t)\mathbf{H}_t^\beta e_t. \tag{3.11}$$

Taking logs of both sides of equation 3.11 gives us:

$$\ln AE_t = -\alpha K_t + \beta \ln \mathbf{H}_t + \ln e_t. \tag{3.12}$$

Then, rewriting equation 3.12 in first difference form, we get:

$$\ln AE_t - \ln AE_{t-1} = -\alpha(K_t - K_{t-1}) + \beta(\ln \mathbf{H}_t - \ln \mathbf{H}_{t-1}) \tag{3.13}$$
$$+ \ln e_t - \ln e_{t-1}.$$

The coefficient $(-\alpha)$ shows the impact of investment in safety capital on the percentage change in the industry's lost workday rate. Following our earlier discussion, we specify the following version of equation 3.13:[8]

$$\ln(LDAY) = \beta_0 + \beta_1 \ln(LDAYLAG) + \beta_2(SAFEINV)$$
$$+ \beta_3 \Delta FSIZE + \beta_4 \Delta \ln(FSIZE)$$
$$+ \beta_5 \Delta \ln(MALE) + \beta_6 \Delta \ln(PROD)$$
$$+ \beta_7 \Delta \ln(UNION) + \beta_8 \Delta \ln(LCR) \tag{3.14}$$
$$+ \beta_9 \Delta \ln(EDUC) + \beta_{10} \Delta \ln(HRE)$$
$$+ \beta_{11} \Delta \ln(NHR) + \beta_{12} \Delta \ln(OT)$$
$$+ \beta_{13} \Delta \ln(CMPLT) + \beta_{14} \Delta \ln(PEN)$$
$$+ \beta_{15} YRDUM + \ln e_t - \ln e_{t-1},$$

where: $LDAY$ = the lost workday rate;
$\Delta FSIZE$ = the change in average firm size;
$\Delta \ln(FSIZE)$ = the change in the log of average firm size;
$\Delta \ln(MALE)$ = the change in the log of percentage male workers;
$\Delta \ln(PROD)$ = the change in the log of percentage production workers;

---

8. To avoid econometric problems that might arise from any serial correlation of errors for the $\ln(LDAY)$ equation, two-step estimation procedure was followed. First, an instrumental variables estimator for $\ln(LDAYLAG)$ was generated, then equation 3.14 was estimated using this first stage variable. This procedure is developed in Griliches (1967) and was previously used by Viscusi (1979b).

$\Delta \ln (UNION)$ = the change in the log of percentage unionized;

$\Delta \ln (LCR)$ = the change in the log of the ratio of labor costs to the value of shipments;

$\Delta \ln (EDUC)$ = the change in the log of average education of the employees;

$\Delta \ln (HRE)$ = the change in the log of average hourly earnings;

$\Delta \ln (NHR)$ = the change in the log of the new hire rate;

$\Delta \ln (OT)$ = the change in the log of average overtime hours;

$\Delta \ln (CMPLT)$ = the change in the log of the rate of worker complaints to OSHA; and

$\Delta \ln (PEN)$ = the change in the log of the industry's penalty rate.

In interpreting the results of estimating equation 3.14, we need to recognize that the McGraw-Hill investment data do not distinguish between safety and health expenditures. While the benefits of safety investment should be almost immediate, health investments will generally not have a prompt effect on workplace injuries as a result of the long lags between onset and realization of the disease. Hence equation 3.14 measures the benefits of combined health and safety investments on *current* injury rates, resulting in an underestimate of the true expected benefits.

Empirical Specifications: OSHA Inspection Activities   Finally, following our earlier paper (Bartel and Thomas 1985), we estimate the following equation for the probability of an OSHA inspection:

$$
\begin{aligned}
\ln INSP = \ \gamma_0 &+ \gamma_1 + \ln (LDAY) + \gamma_2 \ln (SAFEINV) \\
&+ \gamma_3 \ln (PEN) + \gamma_4 (UNION) \\
&+ \gamma_5 \ln (FSIZE) + \gamma_6 \ln (FSIZE) \cdot (YEAR - 74) \\
&+ \gamma_7 \ln (CMPLT) \\
&+ \gamma_8 \ln (CMPLT) \cdot (YEAR - 74) \\
&+ \gamma_9 \ln (PRFT) + \gamma_{10} \ln (DC) \\
&+ \gamma_{11} YRDUM + \mu_3,
\end{aligned}
\tag{3.15}
$$

where the previously undefined variables are

DC = percentage of industry employees in District of Columbia,[9] and

$PRFT$ = (value added minus labor costs) divided by assets.

Our earlier paper did not include *SAFEINV* in the inspection equation.

Results

Equations 3.10, 3.14, and 3.15 are estimated using nonlinear two-stage least squares on a sample of eighteen two-digit manufacturing industries for the time period 1974 through 1978. Hence, we have ninety observations for our pooled cross-section analysis. The results are presented in tables 3.1, 3.2, and 3.3.

The major finding in table 3.1 is the positive and significant effect of OSHA inspections on investments in employee safety and health in the mid-1970s. In 1974, a doubling of the OSHA inspection rate would have produced almost a 90 percent increase in investments in safety and health capital. The negative coefficient on the interaction term between inspections and time indicates, however, that there were diminishing returns to increasing OSHA inspections; in fact, by 1978, a doubling of the inspection rate would have produced only an 18 percent increase in safety investments.

The other coefficients in table 3.1 are all consistent with our predictions. Safety investments are higher when total capital investments (*CAPEXP*) are higher and when the industry is observed to have had a low level of noncompliance with OSHA standards in the previous period (*PENLAG*). As expected, there is no relationship between the accident rate and the level of safety investment. Compliance asymmetries turn out to be quite important. Unionized industries invest less in safety capital because they have already achieved a high preregulation stock of safety capital. In industries with large firms, investment is greater because of economies of scale; this effect occurs primarily in the early years of the time period we are studying, as evidenced by the negative coefficient on the firm size-time interaction term.

Turning to table 3.2, we find that investments in employee

---

9. The *DC* variable is used to control for the fact that workers in the District of Columbia do not have direct representation by a voting member of Congress and hence are incapable of direct political support for OSHA.

safety have produced negative and significant effects on the percentage change in the lost workday rate. Evaluated at the mean level
of safety investments per worker (7.1×10^{-5}), the coefficient on the
SAFEINV variable implies an elasticity for lost workdays with regard
to an investment of 2.1 percent. This elasticity of course implies that
a doubling of prevailing investment levels would at most reduce lost
workdays by 2.1 percent, a remarkably small response.

Finally, in table 3.3, we see that the findings from our earlier
paper (Bartel and Thomas 1985) regarding enforcement asymmetries
are still borne out in the current analysis. Large firms are significantly
less likely to be inspected, especially during the early years of the OSHA
program when small firms had not yet organized themselves to lobby
Congress. The union variable is also negative, as predicted, but is not
significant here. The other important finding in this table is the lack
of any relationship between safety investments and the optimal inspection rate; OSHA's allocation of resources in no way depended on
the rate at which industries were investing in safety capital.

Conclusions

This paper has reexamined OSHA's impact on industrial investments
in employee safety and health. Two previous studies (Viscusi 1979b
and Weidenbaum and de Fina 1978) have argued that OSHA has been
responsible for, respectively, none of and all of these expenditures.
Using data recently revised by McGraw-Hill, we have reanalyzed this
relationship and its resulting costs and benefits.

Our empirical results show that OSHA inspections have had a
positive, sizable, and significant effect on investments in employee
safety and health. Although these investments have had a statistically
negative effect on lost workdays, the magnitude of this effect is extremely small. We can use our coefficients to estimate the costs and
benefits of the investments in employee safety and health that have
been induced by OSHA. First, on the cost side, since total capital spending for United States manufacturing industries in 1977 was $47,459
million,[10] and, according to the McGraw-Hill data, investments in
employee safety and health in manufacturing were approximately 2.7

---

10. This is reported in the Bureau of the Census's *Annual Survey of Manufacturers*.

percent of total capital spending, this implies that $1,281 million was spent by United States manufacturers on employee safety and health capital in that year. According to table 3.1, in 1977, approximately 36 percent of those investments were a result of OSHA inspections, or $461 million. On the benefit side, in 1977, there were 17 million lost workdays in the manufacturing sector,[11] which can be valued at fifty dollars a day,[12] for a total loss of $850 million. Since the elasticity of lost workdays with respect to safety investment is .021 and 36 percent of the safety investments were induced by OSHA enforcement, the benefits attributed to OSHA are $6.4 million. Clearly, the costs of OSHA-induced investments overwhelmingly outweighed the benefits.

Our reexamination of the relationship between OSHA enforcement and industrial investments in employee safety and health supports neither of the previous two studies on this topic. While Viscusi (1979b) argued that none of the investments were attributable to OSHA, and Weidenbaum and de Fina (1978) argued that all were because of OSHA, we find that, on average, about 50 percent were induced by OSHA. Taking a policy perspective, however, we would prefer to stress our findings regarding the very weak relationship between these investments and the lost workday rate. It is because of this weak link that the costs of OSHA-induced investments strongly dominate the benefits of those investments. Stepping up OSHA enforcement efforts would, therefore, not be an appropriate policy. Rather, we would recommend closer study of the true causes of workplace hazards so that industrial investments in safety capital can be more accurately designed.

---

11. There were 20 million manufacturing employees in 1977, and the mean lost workdays per worker reported in our BLS data set is .85.

12. Based on wage data reported in the 1980 *Handbook of Labor Statistics*.

TABLE 3.1
Safety Investment: Two-Stage Nonlinear Least Squares

Independent Variable	Coefficient	t-value
ln (*INSP*)	.893	(1.92)
[ln (*INSP*)] × (*YEAR* − 74)	− .178	(− 1.51)
ln (*CAPEXP*)	.982	(13.01)
ln (*PENLAG*)	− .256	(− 1.50)
ln (*LDAY*)	− .191	(− .89)
ln (*UNION*)	− .559	(− 3.40)
ln (*FSIZE*)	.877	(3.13)
[ln (*FSIZE*)] × (*YEAR* − 74)	− .186	(− 2.32)
D75	− .172	(− .36)
D76	− .570	(− .64)
D77	− .636	(− .46)
D78	− .740	(− .39)
Intercept	− 5.290	(− 2.93)

Notes: dependent variable: ln (*SAFEINV*).
$R^2 = .73$.

TABLE 3.2
Lost Workday Rate: Two-Stage Nonlinear Least Squares

Independent Variable	Coefficient	t-value
ln (*LDAYLAG*)	.966	(62.46)
(*SAFEINV*)	− 295.980	(− 2.02)
Δ ln (*FSIZE*)	.195	(1.00)
Δ *FSIZE*	− .000	(− .10)
Δ ln (*MALE*)	.529	(.41)
Δ ln (*PROD*)	1.210	(.92)
Δ ln (*UNION*)	− .118	(− 1.47)
Δ ln (*LCR*)	− .001	(− .01)
Δ ln (*EDUC*)	.208	(.43)
Δ ln (*HRE*)	.811	(.54)
Δ ln (*NHR*)	− .035	(− .45)
Δ ln (*OT*)	− .210	(− .99)
Δ ln (*CMPLT*)	.051	(1.12)
Δ ln(*PEN*)	.046	(1.80)
D75	.003	(.06)
D76	− .030	(− .55)
D77	− .004	(− .11)
D78	.001	(.01)
Intercept	− .158	(− .89)

Notes: dependent variable: ln (*LDAY*).
$R^2 = .985$.

TABLE 3.3
Probability of OSHA Inspection: Two-Stage Nonlinear Least Squares

Independent Variable	Coefficient	t-value
ln (LDAY)	.461	(9.27)
ln (SAFEINV)	− .005	(− .17)
ln (PEN)	.072	(1.87)
ln (FSIZE)	− .501	(− 12.85)
[ln (FSIZE)] × (YEAR − 74)	.090	(7.74)
ln (UNION)	− .038	(− .83)
ln (CMPLT)	.129	(2.35)
[ln (CMPLT)] × (YEAR − 74)	.124	(6.92)
ln (PRFT)	.556	(3.98)
ln (DC)	− .097	(− 3.91)
D75	.496	(3.42)
D76	.435	(1.57)
D77	.676	(1.70)
D78	.861	(1.66)
Intercept	.523	(.74)

Notes: dependent variable: ln (INSP).
R^2 = .97.

4·BENEFITS AND CLAIM DURATION

John D. Worrall and Richard J. Butler

Over the last fifteen years the growth of the absolute and relative (to other forms of compensation) cost of the workers' compensation system has been a stimulus to actuarial and economic research on this important social insurance program. In this chapter we present evidence on a hitherto neglected aspect of the program, namely, the effect that changes in the benefit structure have on the average duration that an individual is expected to receive workers' compensation benefits. We review the appropriate statistical models for estimating such a relation, given that the data on disability spells may be incomplete (right-censored data), and present estimates for the single most important claim type under workers' compensation, the low back claim. We focus on temporary total disability claims because we expect these to reflect economic incentives more readily than claims that are permanently incapacitating. We find that the expected length of stay on workers' compensation is significantly affected by changes in the benefits, wages, and other major parameters of the workers' compensation process, including the representation of the claimant by a lawyer.

We thank David Durbin and R. McAuley for programming and research assistance, and the Actuarial Committee of the National Council on Compensation Insurance and Philip Borba for helpful comments—J.D.W. and D.A.

To gain some perspective on the importance of our duration estimates, consider the cost of workers' compensation to a representative worker. The expected cost to the system for the representative worker of the ith claim type is the probability of filing a claim of the ith type, P_i, times the average duration of the claim given that one files, D_i, times the average benefit per period of claim type i, B_i. Summing over claim types yields the expected costs for a representative worker under the workers' compensation system. This relationship is illustrated by equation 4.1:

$$\text{costs} = \sum_i P_i D_i B_i, \tag{4.1}$$

where "costs" are the expected per capita costs of workers' compensation.

Simple manipulation shows that for small changes, the percentage change in expected costs, or the change in the natural logarithm of costs, "dln," can be decomposed into percentage changes in the component costs as:

$$\text{dln costs} = \sum_i S_i (\text{dln} P_i + \text{dln} D_i + \text{dln} B_i), \tag{4.2}$$

where S_i is the cost share of each injury type. That is, the percentage change in cost equals a weighted average of the percentage change in the probability of filing a claim, the percentage change in the average duration of a claim, and the percentage change in benefits. The weights, S_i, are the relative cost shares of each kind of claim and sum to one.

One can isolate the source of the recent cost inflation in workers' compensation by using this relationship. For example, there is a simple direct effect that a change in the benefit structure induces; a 10 percent increase for all benefits, holding the claim rates and average duration constant, simply implies a 10 percent increase in the cost per employee. However, an increase in benefits may also induce changes in the duration of a claim of any given type as well as increase the probability of filing the claim of any given type. For example, the research of Chelius (1974), Butler (1983), and Butler and Worrall (1983), and Worrall and Appel (1982) shows that benefits have had a significant, indirect effect on costs, in addition to their direct impact, because as benefits rise, they appear to induce a rise in the probability of filing an indemnity claim. Hence, a 10 percent increase in benefits may be expected to have more than a 10 percent increase in total expected cost per claim since it also affects the probability of filing a claim. An uninvestigated area of research in workers' compensation concerns what impact a change in benefits would have on the expected duration of any given claim type. Our research represents an initial effort to examine how the duration of a claim is affected by the size of benefits.[1]

The problem looks easy enough: if one has data on the duration of claims, why not simply regress it on a number of independent variables and see what this implies? Indeed, the conventional search theory in economics suggests the variables that ought to be included as regressors on the right-hand side of such an equation. For example, the probability of leaving the workers' compensation status once one begins to receive benefits depends upon the probability that an expected wage offer exceeds one's reservation wage, that is,

$$\text{Prob (expected wage offer} > \text{reservation wage).} \tag{4.3}$$

Note that the expected wage offer is the probability of receiving the wage offer times the wage that one receives, given receipt of such an offer. The reservation wage is determined by the value of one's time and represents the minimum payment a claimant accepts to leave the workers' compensation disability status. Therefore, the duration of a claim should decrease as the wage offer or the probability of a wage offer increases, and increase with increases in the reservation wage.

We have proxies for these variables. We approximate the probability of a wage offer with a measure of the expected probability that an employee will be able to return to his or her previous work. We capture this return to previous work probability by controlling for the

---

1. In a companion paper (Butler and Worrall 1985), we discuss some related estimation issues when estimating a hazard in the presence of worker heterogeneity (unobserved) and present full information maximum likelihood techniques when the distribution of time is parametrically specified. The advantage of the proportional hazard rate used here is that the estimates are robust with respect to the actual distribution of time. For related work on the British system of sick leave, see Fenn (1981). Fenn also finds that as the generosity of sick pay increases, there is an increase in the duration of illnesses. Worrall and Appel (1982) used a simple reduced form to examine the effect of changes in the replacement ratio on aggregate claim severity.

claimant's employment status at the time the claim was filed.[2] The wage offer is best approximated by the actual wage received before injury. We approximate the reservation wage with the weekly benefits under the workers' compensation system. Hence, if one regressed the logarithm of duration on these variables, one would expect to see a negative relationship between the probability of receiving a wage offer or the pre-injury wage and the length of duration on a workers' compensation claim. On the other hand, an increase in the workers' compensation benefits should increase the expected duration as it lowers the opportunity cost of remaining out of employment. We also attempt to control for other demographic variables, severity of injury, and other institutional factors by either including them directly in the analysis or by partitioning the data along these lines.

However, a problem still remains with our log duration regression if the data that we use to estimate this function turn out to be censored. We shall explain this problem in more detail.

NCCI's Claim Survey

The data come from the detailed claim call survey developed by the Actuarial Committee of the National Council on Compensation Insurance (NCCI). In April 1979, insurance companies began forwarding a random sample of claims filed in each of the twelve participating states to NCCI. Data were gathered on sex; age; pre-injury wage; injury date; whether the employee was a regular employee, unemployed because of a plant shutdown, on strike, or retired; type of claim; hospital days; weekly benefit; whether the claimant was represented by a lawyer, and if so, the amount of court expenditures; and so on. The random sample is longitudinal. If a claimant continues to receive benefits, reports on the status of the claim are filed at 6-, 18-, 30-, and 42-month intervals. Although most claimants complete their disability spells in less than six months and generate only one claim

---

2. We have created a regular employment status dummy variable. The value of the variable is one if, at the time the claim was filed, the claimant was a regular employee. The unemployed, those on layoff or on strike, retired employees, and so on were recorded as a zero on this dummy variable. Since the likelihood of a job opportunity is much greater for regular employees than for other employees, we feel that this is an excellent proxy for the probability of a wage offer—certainly much better than the often used alternative, a measure of the local labor market unemployment rate.

report, many other claimants remain on workers' compensation. Observations on claimants who have not completed their tenure on workers' compensation are right-censored.

These right-censored observations pose a problem. If we omit them we may be losing valuable information about the sample distribution. Moreover, these observations may be right censored because they represent the claims of workers whose benefit receipt typically lasts longer than that of workers whose claims are closed. Discarding information on open claims is likely to lead to a biased sample. Alternatively, if we include observations that are right censored and use ordinary least squares regression techniques, we obviously also get biased results, because we will be treating these censored observations on the same basis that we treat other observations that are complete in the sample. What we need are techniques that control for right censoring,[3] as well as duration dependence, that is, the longer one is on a workers' compensation claim, the more (positive duration dependence) or less (negative duration dependence) likely one is to leave claim status.

Hazard Rate Estimation

The secret to solving the censoring problem is to create a variable that determines both whether one leaves workers' compensation as well as the length of time one stays on workers' compensation. Estimators of these types, called hazard rates, have been applied by economists to problems of finding the determinants of unemployment duration and welfare dependence. They have been used frequently in medical statistical applications. The hazard rate is the instantaneous rate of change from one state to another. It is a conditional probability. A classic example is, "what is the probability that a light bulb will burn out in the next small interval, given that it has survived to time t?" The hazard rate can be written as

$$\lambda(t) = \lim_{dt \to 0} \frac{Pr(t < T < t + dt \quad T > t)}{dt}. \tag{4.4}$$

---

3. In our sample, about a third of the observations were right censored—indicating strong potential for biased estimates when the censoring is not taken into account.

Equation 4.4 can be rewritten as

$$\lambda(t) = \frac{f(t)}{1 - F(t)} \tag{4.5}$$

where f is a probability density function and F is the distribution function. The survivor function is $[1 - F(t)]$, the probability of not having changed states by time t, since $F(t)$ is the distribution function that corresponds to the probability of an event occurring. In our empirical work, this event is leaving workers' compensation status at any point in time. We wish to choose a specific parameterization for the hazard rate, $\lambda(t)$, letting it vary as wages, benefits, and other characteristics of the respondents vary. Once we have estimated the parameters corresponding to our socioeconomic variables, we can calculate the relative impact that each has on the duration of a claim. If we fully specify $F(t)$, we can also calculate the estimated duration of a claim as it relates to the socioeconomic variables by adding up the probability of having survived to that moment. That is, we add up all the probabilities of having remained on workers' compensation status to time t in order to get the expected duration. Accordingly, we parameterize $\lambda(t)$ as a function of the variables of interest, including pre-injury wage, benefit, employment status, and other sociodemographic information, and then translate the results into the expected duration of claimants' spells on workers' compensation.

Two Hazard Approaches

There are two types of hazard rates that can be estimated. The first type is dependent upon an explicit distribution of time $F(t)$. From equation 4.5, we can see that a given distribution for $F(t)$ implies a specific form for the hazard rate. In a companion paper (Butler and Worrall 1985) we take this first approach in order to control for potential unobserved heterogeneity across claims. The drawbacks from specifying a specific $F(t)$ for the data, however, are that the $F(t)$ chosen may be misspecified and lead to erroneous conclusions, and the full information maximum likelihood programs are not only costly but must in general be tailored for each different $F(t)$ chosen.

Another approach, the one adopted here, is based upon an important paper by Cox (1972) on the problem of estimating hazard rates in the biostatistics literature. This alternative parameterization is given as

$$\lambda_i(t) = \lambda(t) \exp(X \cdot \beta), \tag{4.6}$$

where we use the subscript i to indicate that the hazard rate for each individual has a common component term $\lambda(t)$, whose function does not vary across individuals but can be any (separable) function of time. The "exp $(X \cdot \beta)$" term is a shift factor that depends upon each individual's sociodemographic characteristics. Cox showed that there are essentially distribution-free methods of estimating the shift coefficients, β, and hence of retrieving the impact of the regressors on the hazard rate. We can rewrite the hazard rate in logarithmic form as

$$\log \lambda_i(t) = \log \lambda(t) + X\beta \tag{4.7}$$

Cox's method essentially cancels out the $\log \lambda(t)$ function common to all spells and estimates β independently of the distribution for time implied by $\lambda(t)$ on the right-hand side. The cost of this generality, as we note below, is that we can only calculate the relative effect of each of the X's on the expected duration. Since we do not know what the distribution of time $[F(t)]$ is, we cannot calculate the expected duration without extraneous information. The β's of the proportional hazard rate model of equation 4.7 are given in table 4.1.

The specification in table 4.1 in column 1 is based on an important paper by Fenn (1981). Fenn's analysis is most similar to our own, although his focuses on any kind of sick pay rather than on workers' compensation. Fenn's data come from a general survey of British workers, whereas ours are from a sample of United States workers insured under the workers' compensation system. Fenn estimated proportional hazard rate variables including those in column 1, except that, instead of employment status for the individual, Fenn has the local employment rate. Fenn also included other demographic variables in his data that we do not have available in our data. These variables (the number of children, the number of full-time employees, work experience, and the two occupational dummies) were all statistically insignificant in his analysis. We hope, therefore, that our exclusion of them will not seriously bias our results.

In the first column we capture the impact of the sick pay with the natural logarithm of the replacement ratio. In Fenn's analysis, the replacement ratio was the ratio of sick pay, Social Security, and of private insurance, relative to the total weekly wage that one was receiving prior to going on disability status. In our case, this is the wages that are replaced by workers' compensation benefits. Like Fenn we find that this variable is statistically significant and negative, indicating that the higher the benefits are relative to forgone wages, the less likely one is to leave disability, and, hence, the longer will be the expected duration of the claim. The interpretation of the other variables is also straightforward. The logarithm of the injury age captures such things as changes in taste over time, and especially changes in the expected value of future wages should the individual return to the work force. Since the older one is, the shorter the subsequent stream of wages upon returning to work, we expect age to decrease the hazard rate. The estimated negative sign is as expected and consistent with the results of Fenn's analysis. Hospital days represent a measure of severity in our analysis and, like Fenn, we find that the more severe the injury, the longer will be the duration of disability. Finally, we have included in all our runs a marital status dummy variable: it takes the value of one if individuals are married but zero otherwise. We find that marriage tends to decrease the transition rate from workers' compensation to work status, and, consequently, it will increase the expected duration of a stay in the nonwork state. The negative impact may reflect the dominance of a secondary worker effect, that is, a working wife (we have only males in our sample) can support the family should the husband be disabled. Apparently, this effect dominates any single breadwinner effects in the sample that would tend to cause married men to return to work sooner. In column 2, we augment this specification with a variable indicating whether or not a lawyer represented the workers' compensation claimant. As indicated there, this is highly (statistically) significant and negative, suggesting that when a lawyer represents a claimant, the length of stay on workers' compensation will tend to increase since the transition rate from workers' compensation decreases.

The problem with the specifications in columns 1 and 2 is that they essentially restrict the benefit and wage variables to similar magnitudes but opposite signs. This restriction is relaxed in our preferred specification, presented in column 3, where the wage and benefit variables are entered separately in the regression. Note that the other coefficients are not significantly affected by the relaxing of the restriction imposed in columns 1 and 2. Indeed, the restriction in columns 1 and 2 may not have been unreasonable, as the wage and benefit coefficients have the expected sign and appear to be of similar magnitude. That is, an increase in wages, which represents the expected wage offer should the individual be able to return to work, increases the hazard rate and hence would be expected to decrease the duration that a worker remains on workers' compensation. The employment status variable, a proxy for the probability of a wage offer, is also consistent with the expected wage offer/search explanation. The coefficient of the benefit variable is significantly negative and indicates that an increase in benefits will decrease the transition rate and, therefore, increase the expected duration of the workers' compensation spell. Columns 4, 5, and 6 represent alternative specifications of the model, and are presented to show how the robustness of the model varies with the exclusion of other regressors. The model chi-square statistics indicate that all of the models represented here are statistically significant at the usual levels.

Implications

In table 4.2 we have listed the variables as they were entered into the proportional hazard rate models. We have calculated both their mean values and the elasticities of expected duration with respect to these various regressor variables. Recall that since we are using a proportional hazard rate model, we do not know the expected duration because the proportional hazard rate model allows time to enter in any arbitrary way as long as it is separable from the **X** vector. We have estimated the vector of socioeconomic effects, β, independently of the distribution of time. We do not know the distribution of time and cannot calculate expected duration without additional information. So we assume the distribution is one of the most commonly used functions whose hazard rate is separable in time, namely, the Weibull distribution, and use the observed mean duration rather than the expected mean duration. Use of the Weibull provides the additional information we need to calculate the effect that each of the variables will have on the expected mean duration of a claim.

We present two simulations in table 4.2. The first corresponds to the case where the duration of the claim has no effect on the hazard rate (implying that $F(t)$ is an exponential function, a restricted form of the Weibull distribution). There is no duration dependence in the sense that the probability of leaving a workers' compensation claim is independent of how long one has been receiving such benefits. The second is the case where the duration of a claim affects the hazard rate negatively. We have assumed $F(t)$ is Weibull for both cases. The first row—based on the specification in column 1 of table 4.1 which includes the replacement ratio—implies a 2 to 4 percent increase in the average number of weeks on a claim whenever the replacement rate increases by 10 percent. This brackets the unconstrained wage and benefit effects given in the next two rows that are based on our preferred specification in table 4.1. As indicated in the parentheses in the third row, a 10 percent increase in benefits could increase the average claim duration by 1.5 and 3.5 days. Clearly, this indirect impact of an increase in benefits is not trivial: benefits increasing by 10 percent will increase expected costs by at least 14 percent—the direct 10 percent impact of benefits plus a 4 percent increase induced by the lengthening duration of claims. Relative to the wage, benefit, and probability of wage offer effects, the sociodemographic variables are less significant.

The results for the duration dependence simulation in the far right-hand column show even more pronounced benefit and wage elasticities. Indeed, for a hazard rate elasticity of -0.5, we find that a 10 percent increase in wages implies ultimately at least a 19 percent increase in the costs of low back claims, since the average duration increase induced by the change of benefits is 9 percent.[4] Clearly, while the caveats given above must be borne in mind, these duration effects are large enough to warrant further research into this neglected area of study in workers' compensation—extending this analysis to other

---

4. If we write the Weibull distribution function as

$$F(t) = 1 - \exp[-(t/b)^c],$$

where b and c are parameters (b is the scale parameter), then the hazard rate, given in equation 4.7, is the result of letting

$$\gamma = c, \text{ and}$$
$$b = (\gamma/\exp(X\beta))^{1/\gamma}.$$

Clearly, if $\beta_1 > 0$ (the ith element in the β vector of coefficients), and $\gamma > 0$, then

$$\frac{\partial b}{\partial x_i} < 0.$$

injury types as well as to other states in the NCCI sample. The results of our initial study of the United States work injury system bear the same implicit message as Fenn's study of the British system. There is incentive response to benefit change in the system. Our research leads us to believe that this incentive response is strong.[5]

Consider equation 4.2, presented earlier. It illustrated that the change in the cost of workers' compensation could be decomposed into three components: a claim frequency or probability of claim filing effect; a severity or duration of workers' compensation spell effect; and a benefit increase effect. The effect of a benefit increase is obvious. If the benefit is raised by 10 percent, the cost of all new claims increases by 10 percent relative to costs at the old benefit level. However, if there are induced frequency and severity effects, the cost increases generated by legislatively mandated benefit increases can far exceed the 10 percent benefit increase. Elsewhere (Butler and Worrall 1983) we present evidence that a 10 percent increase in workers' compensation benefits induces a 4 percent increase in indemnity claim frequency. As benefits are increased, workers may have more incentive to file claims, less incentive to be careful on the job, or more incentive to bear additional risk on the job. Consider a labor market generating 100 claims with a benefit index of 100. If legislatures, in a search for benefit adequacy, increase the benefit level to an index level of 110, we would expect to see 104 claims and a cost increase of 14.4 percent. The research we have presented above, however, indicates that the employee response does not end with increased claim filing. Employees lengthen their disability spells as well.

Our model of employee response with a hazard rate elasticity assumption of -0.5 implies that the length of spells attributable to

---

Since the mean of the Weibull distribution is $b\Gamma_e[(c+1)/c]$, an increase in the hazard rate as a result of a change in X_i (when $\beta_i > 0$) will decrease the average time that a claimant will stay on compensation status. Since $f(t)$ for the Weibull is

$$f(t) = \frac{ct^{c-1}}{b^c}\exp[-(t/b)^c],$$

the log of the hazard rate is

$$\log\lambda(t) = (\gamma-1)\ln t + \chi\beta.$$

5. In our companion paper, we find a hazard rate elasticity of $-.11$, which brackets the simulations given in table 4.2. These results also appear to hold when more complicated distributions of time are appropriate. See Butler and Worrall (1985).

low back injuries increase by 9 percent when benefits are increased by 10 percent. This does not mean that the ultimate impact of a 10.0 percent benefit increase is to increase costs by 24.7 percent (i.e., 1.10 × 1.04 × 1.09 = 1.247).

Disability is a flexible state. It may be easier for employees who are temporarily incapacitated to exhibit incentive response as the opportunity cost of their time changes than for employees who are permanently disabled. Similarly, it may be easier for employees to extend their nonwork spells when the nature of the injury makes monitoring difficult. Given that temporary total disability spells as a result of low back injury could fall into both of these categories, the 9 percent increase in length of spell may be an upper bound to employee response. As noted, however, we have used other distributions and explicit heterogeneity controls, and come to the same conclusion (Butler and Worrall 1985). Employees lengthen their disability spells when benefits are increased.

TABLE 4.1
Proportional Hazard Rate Model:
Temporary Total Low Back Cases for Males (Illinois)

Variable	(1) BETA	(2) BETA	(3) BETA	(4) BETA	(5) BETA	(6) BETA
LN replace rate	−.4496* (.1213) (.0002)	−.4044* (.1230) (.0010)				
LN wage			.2953* (.1319) (.0252)	.3706* (.1304) (.0045)		
LN benefit			−.4631* (.1229) (.0002)	−.4948* (.1224) (.0001)	−.2412* (.0815) (.0031)	−.2103* (.0822) (.0105)
LN injury age	−.0903 (.1125) (.4065)	−.1875 (.1136) (.0987)	−.1411 (.1153) (.2211)	−.0572 (.1147) (.6181)	−.1182 (.1139) (.2992)	−.0261 (.1129) (.8169)
Hospital days	−.1173* (0.126) (.0000)	−.1151* (.0127) (.0000)	−.1163* (.0128) (.0000)	−.1179* (.1026) (.0000)	−.1170* (.0128) (.0000)	−.1184* (.0126) (.0000)
Employment status	.4046 (.2077) (.0514)	.3823 (.2076) (.0655)	.3624 (.2079) (.0813)	.3907 (.2079) (.0603)	.3122 (.2038) (.1255)	.3395 (.2039) (.0959)
Lawyer		−1.9140* (.2933) (.0000)	−1.9309* (.2935) (.0000)		−1.9545* (.2933) (.0000)	
Married	−.2364* (.0824) (.0041)	−.1792* (.0827) (.0302)	−.1537 (.0841) (.0676)	−.2196* (.0835) (.0086)	−.1434 (.0838) (.0871)	−.2077* (.0833) (.0127)
−2 log L	9694.93	9612.71	9609.07	9692.91	9639.83	9726.80
Model chi-square	180.07*	262.29*	265.93*	182.09*	262.18*	175.21*
D.F.	5	6	7	6	6	5
PROB	0.0	0.0	0.0	0.0	0.0	0.0

Notes: The first line under the estimated coefficients is the standard error; the second line is the probability significance level of the estimated coefficient.

TABLE 4.2

Expected Duration Elasticities Based on the Proportional Hazard Rate
Model (change in weeks[c] when X changes by 10%)

Variable (X)	Mean	No Duration Dependence	Duration Dependence
		$\dfrac{\partial \ln\lambda}{\partial \ln t} = 0$	$\dfrac{\partial \ln\lambda}{\partial \ln t} = -\dfrac{1}{2}$
LN (Replacement Rate)[a]	− .460	.187 (.10 weeks)	.374 (.2)
LN (Wages)[b]	5.696	− .295 (− .20 weeks)	− .590 (.3)
LN (Benefit)[b]	5.235	.463 (.20 weeks)	.926 (.5)
LN (Injury Age)[b]	3.493	.141 (.10 weeks)	.282 (.1)
Hospital Days[b]	1.408	.164 (.10 weeks)	.328 (.2)
Employment Status[b]	.964	− .349 (− .20 weeks)	− .698 (− .4)
Lawyer[b]	.043	.083 (.04 weeks)	.166 (.1)
Married[b]	.702	.108 (.10 weeks)	.216 (.1)

Notes: All elasticities reported assume exponential and Weibull distributions for time.

a. This Elasticity is based on the model in table 4.1, column 2.

b. These elasticities are based on the model in table 4.1, column 3.

c. The calculations in parentheses are based on the observed mean duration (5.16 weeks) rather than the expected mean duration (the latter cannot be calculated without the full maximum likelihood estimates of a specified functional form). Hence, these could overstate or understate the actual change in weeks. However, our preliminary work, based on a full information maximum likelihood Weibull estimate indicates that the expected mean duration is twelve weeks.

5 · EXPERIENCE RATING AND WORKPLACE SAFETY

Richard B. Victor

Workers' compensation insurance is the primary source of compensation for injured workers in the United States.[1] Statutes require employers to provide mandated benefits to their workers who suffer work-related disabilities. But the workers' compensation system does much more than provide injured workers with needed financial support. By imposing part of the costs of injuries on the employer, it conveys financial incentives to induce them to prevent workplace injuries and diseases. It conveys these incentives directly to firms that self-insure and through merit rating of insurance premiums for insured firms. This chapter examines the financial incentives provided by the workers' compensation system through experience rating, a common form of merit rating.[2] We use a simulation model based on the rating formulas commonly used in most states.

Over the past decade, three national study panels were convened. All debated the nature and adequacy of workers' compensation prevention incentives (National Commission 1972; Interagency Task Force on Workplace Safety and Health 1978; Interdepartmental Workers' Compensation Task Force 1977; Russell 1973 and 1974). All offered proposals to enhance these incentives: raising benefits,

---

1. The material presented herein relies heavily on Victor (1983).
2. The primary purpose of merit rating is to define an appropriate price for a specific insured. But in doing so, the procedures reward safer insureds and penalize riskier ones—creating incentives to be safer.

extending experience rating, and mandating deductibles, for example. The debates and deliberations of these study panels have produced three now widely accepted propositions about the workers' compensation prevention incentives: first, that they are inadequate; second, that self-insureds have the maximum incentives and that insurance can only serve to dilute them; and third, that raising workers' compensation benefits will generally increase employer incentives.

We first review the important features of the experience-rating formulas. Second, we outline the basic structure and features of the simulation model of prevention incentives used in this analysis. Third, we reexamine these commonly accepted propositions using the simulation model.[3] Finally, we illustrate several important uses of the model.

Experience Rating

Workers' compensation insurance premiums are based upon what are called *manual* or *class insurance* rates. These are the rates applicable to a specific industry or occupational group. For instance, the average California sawmill pays almost 10 percent of its production employee payroll for workers' compensation insurance. Experience rating is a way of modifying these class rates to take into account the specific firm's injury history or experience. If the firm's experience is better than average for a firm of its size and class, its premiums will be reduced. If the firm's experience is worse than the average, its premiums will be increased.

The experience modification factor, which is applied to adjust the class insurance rates, is merely the weighted average of the firm's experience and the class experience, relative to the class experience. The weights are determined by the actuarial credibility, or reliability, of a firm's own experience. The greater this credibility, the more weight given to the firm's own loss experience. This credibility, in turn, depends upon the total expected losses for a typical firm in that class—which are based on the firm's payroll and actuarially derived class-expected loss rates. The credibility factors are the same for all firms in a given class that have the same payroll. Total expected losses—the credibility of a firm's own experience—will increase with

---

3. For a detailed description of the simulation model, see Victor (1983).

firm size, the hazardousness of the industry, and wage scale. The greater the total expected losses, the greater weight given to the firm's own experience and the less weight given to class experience. At the extremes, a very small firm in a not very hazardous industry may have its premium entirely determined by the class rates. If so, this firm is *class rated*. At the other extreme, a firm may be sufficiently large, or in a sufficiently hazardous industry, that its experience modification factor is entirely determined by its own experience. This firm is called *self-rated*.

The Simulation Model

We define the experience-rated workers' compensation prevention incentive as the present value of the dollars saved in future premiums from the prevention of a given claim. Computationally, it is merely the product of change in the experience modification factor, owing to the prevention or occurrence of a given claim, the firm's payroll, and its class insurance rate. The greater the credibility of a firm's loss experience, the more sensitive are its premiums to its own loss experience and the larger is the prevention incentive.

The simulation model computes the prevention incentive as defined above for the prevention of a specific claim, given the characteristics of the firm, state workers' compensation benefit levels, and insurance rates and rating parameters in actual use.

The experience-rating formulas lie at the heart of the model. While these formulas have similar elements and structures across states, the rating parameters may vary. To illustrate the development of the simulation model, we present the version appropriate for the thirty-eight states that use the NCCI formulas.

Through experience rating, an insurer seeks to forecast future losses and reflect them in an insured's premium. It does so by reference to a firm's prior loss experience. The insurer applies a firm-specific "experience modification factor" (ϵ) to the industry class average insurance rate, called the manual rate (MR), to determine the firm's premium (π):

$$\pi = \epsilon \times MR \times PAY \times (1 - PD). \qquad (5.1)$$

Since the manual rate is stated as a percentage of payroll (actually, per \$100 of payroll), the experience-adjusted manual rate is multiplied by the firm's payroll (*PAY*) to give the gross premium. Larger insureds often receive premium discounts (*PD*) to account for the lower costs of acquiring and servicing their business.[4] These discounts increase with the size of the insured, ranging up to 16.3 percent. Because acquisition costs tend to differ systematically between stock and mutual insurance companies, premium discounts differ commensurately.[5]

For the largest firms, ϵ is merely the ratio of actual to class average losses.[6] If actual losses are greater than expected losses, ϵ is greater than 1 and the premium rate exceeds the manual rate. If actual losses are smaller than average, the reverse is true.

A larger firm, whose loss experience is sufficiently credible that its experience modification is based entirely on its own loss experience, is called *self-rated*. The loss experience of medium- and smaller-size firms is not fully reliable actuarially as a predictor of their future loss experience. It would be like generalizing from a small sample: the smaller the sample, the less reliable the generalizations. In formulating predictions, the experience-rating formula gives some weight to both the firm's actual losses and the class average losses. The greater the weight of a firm's own experience, the greater the "extent of experience rating," and the more sensitive are premiums to losses. The size of future "expected losses" determines the relative weights on firm and industry experience.[7] Larger expected losses increase the credibility of the firm's own experience; as a result, the formula assigns it greater weight.

Examining the experience-rating formula used by the NCCI makes this clear:

$$\epsilon = [A_p + WA_e + (1 - W)E_e + B]/(E_t + B), \tag{5.2}$$

where A_p = actual primary losses;

4. California allows no premium discounts. Instead, dividends paid to insureds at the completion of the policy year tend to be larger than in other states.

5. Stock companies offer greater discounts than nonstock companies. However, the latter often pay ex post dividend to policy holders.

6. "Expected losses" means the losses one would expect on average for a hypothetical firm with a given payroll in a given industry. It ignores the specific firm's loss experience in deriving expectations.

7. "Expected losses" does not refer to the specific firm's expected losses but to an "average" firm's expected losses, when the average firm has the same payroll as the firm for which the ϵ is being computed, and is in the same class and state.

A_e = actual excess losses;

E_e = expected excess losses;

W = credibility weight on actual losses;

B = ballast factor to reduce sensitivity in smaller firms; and

E_t = total expected losses.

The preponderance of states use this formula, although specific values will vary from state to state. Calculation of the experience modification factor (ϵ) uses loss and payroll data from three prior years, lagged one year. For example, the 1984 computation is based on losses and payroll from 1980, 1981, and 1982.

Notice that actual losses are divided into two components: primary (A_p) and excess (A_e). All individual losses below \$2,000 are primary losses. Above that, a formula divides each loss between primary and excess losses so that as losses increase, the relative importance of primary losses declines[8] (see table 5.1). The calculation of the experience modification factor includes the entire primary loss component of each loss. Thus, for a given firm, premiums are more sensitive to small losses than larger losses. Significantly, smaller losses constitute the majority of workers' compensation claims.

The excess loss component also enters directly into the experience modification computation, although its importance depends upon the weight given to the firm's own loss experience—the W value in equation 5.2. This W value varies from 0 to 1, increasing with total expected losses. Table 5.2 provides illustrative values for Georgia, Oregon, and North Carolina. The table clearly shows how the extent of experience rating can vary across states.[9] The "speed" at which the extent of experience rating increases varies from state to state.

Three factors determine total expected losses: the industry expected loss rate (ELR), the firm's average salary (S), and the number of employees in the firm (L):

$$E_t = ELR \times S \times L. \tag{5.3}$$

---

8. In the NCCI states, the formula used is $A_p = (1,000 \times L) \div (8,000 + L)$, where L is the actual loss.

9. Interstate differences in state average wage levels and industry loss experience explain the major differences in table 5.2. Consider otherwise identical firms in three states that pay the same proportion of their states' average wage and are in industries with the same expected loss rate. The firms will have different expected losses but the same W value.

Because the tables use expected losses over the three-year experience-rated period, E_t must be multiplied by 3. The expected loss rate reflects the industry's (but not an individual firm's) loss experience: frequency, severity, and benefit levels. It varies from industry to industry and state to state. Total expected losses (hence, W; hence, the extent of experience rating) will be greater where, *ceteris paribus*, the industry is more hazardous, the state is more liberal, the firm's average wage is greater, or the firm is larger.

For firms whose loss experience is not fully credible ($W < 1$), the formula also gives some weight to industry average (or expected) excess losses (E_e). The ϵ for any firm is merely the weighted average of the firm's and industry's loss experience, with the weights depending on the credibility of the firm's loss experience.

B is a balancing factor that declines to 0 as E_t grows. It serves to reduce the sensitivity of the ϵ in smaller firms to fluctuations in losses. It also influences the extent of experience rating for both primary and excess loss components. Smaller B values mean greater sensitivity of premiums to losses. By contrast, W affects only the excess loss component.

For the largest (self-rated) firms, $W = 1$ and $B = 0$. Here, the ϵ formula reduces to the ratio of actual to expected losses. The greater the expected losses are, the more sensitive the firm's premiums will be to its loss experience.

Computing Experience-Rated Prevention Savings

Under experience rating, actions to reduce losses will save future insurance premiums. Because insurers base the ϵ computation on three years' prior data, current prevention yields savings in three years. We can compute the resulting savings directly from the ϵ formula. We begin by assuming that, without additional prevention, the firm expects its loss experience in future years to be identical to past years. As a result, its future ϵ in any given year would be unchanged (ϵ_1), as shown in equation 5.4:

$$\epsilon_1 = A_p + WA_e + (1 - W)E_e + B / (E_t + B). \tag{5.4}$$

Its premium in that year (π_1) would be:

$$\pi_1 = \epsilon_1 \times MR \times PAY \times (1 - PD). \tag{5.5}$$

Now we assume that the firm sets out on a new course of prevention that will most likely forestall one claim of amount η.[10] Prevention reduces primary and excess losses by their appropriate shares of η (A_p^{η}, A_e^{η}). The new post-prevention experience modification factor (ϵ^*) becomes:

$$\epsilon^* = (A_p - A_p^*) + W(A_e - A_e)$$
$$+ (1 - W)E_e + B / (E_t + B), \tag{5.6}$$

where $A_p^* A_e^*$ are the total primary and excess components, adjusting for the prevented claim (η). The firm's premium falls to:

$$\pi^* = \epsilon^* \times MR \times PAY \times (1 - PD). \tag{5.7}$$

Since ϵ^* is less than ϵ_1, π^* is less than π_1.

The savings from prevention are, of course, the difference between pre- and post-prevention premiums ($\Delta\pi = \pi_1 - \pi^*$); that is,

$$\Delta\pi = [A_p\eta + WA_e\eta]/[E_t + B] \times MR \times PAY \times (1 - PD). \tag{5.8}$$

Whereas the savings from prevention for the self-insured firm are simply the workers' compensation benefits and claims adjustment expenses that are avoided, for the experience-rated firm, the savings are determined by a complex interaction of factors. These interactions make generalizations difficult; yet we shall see that the experience-rated savings from prevention increase, all else being equal, with

the size of the loss;
firm size;
industry hazardousness;
liberality of the state's benefit rules and administrative practices;
the firm's wage scale; and
the ratio of the manual rate to the expected loss rate.

The *safety key ratio*, the ratio of the manual rate to the expected loss rate, deserves additional explanation. Its significance is most clearly seen for the large, self-rated firms (where $W = 1$, $B = 0$). Here the

---

10. Prevention will probably reduce the probability of a variety of consequences. For the risk-neutral firm, the monetary value of the difference between the pre- and post-prevention mean consequences will determine the financial incentive. This difference is a more rigorous interpretation for η. Strictly speaking, the value change in each probability consequence would be fed through the ϵ formula, as described above, and then summed.

financial incentives can be expressed as

$$\Delta\pi = [\eta/(ELR \times PAY)] \times MR \times PAY \times (1 - PD). \qquad (5.9)$$

Before applying the premium discount, this reduces to $\Delta\pi = \eta \times (MR/ELR)$.[11]

The prevention savings for self-rated firms is the actual loss (η) multiplied by the safety key ratio. Currently, this ratio typically varies between 2 and 3. Thus self-rated firms would save two to three times the actual loss prevented. This savings accrues over a three-year period.

The denominator of this ratio—the expected loss rate—is computed from historical loss data. It reflects only losses incurred, valued at the time incurred, and omits related expenses. The numerator— the manual rate—is forward looking. It attempts to predict the future value of both claims and expenses. Thus it includes an adjustment for trends in benefit levels and utilization. It also includes an adjustment for open claims whose ultimate cost is uncertain, known as a *loss development factor*. Finally, it includes insurance company expenses and profits. This, the size of the safety key ratio reflects three things: insurance company expenses, trends in benefits and utilization, and loss development.

If there were no open claims, and benefits and utilization did not change over time, the key ratio would be completely determined by the expense component in the insurance rates. Includable expenses vary from state to state but typically are 30 to 40 percent of the manual rate. Table 5.3 presents the key ratios for different expense loadings in this range. Even if trends and loss development were ignored, a self-rated insured employer would save more from prevention than a similar self-insured employer.[12] This does not necessarily mean that the actual expenses of adjusting a single claim are greater for insureds than for self-insureds. The insurance rates load average adjustment

---

11. For simplicity, we assume static labor force and wage levels. To the extent that wages or employment are growing, the insured incentives described may be greater than depicted.

12. Because experience-rated savings occur in the future, while self-insured savings accrue in the current period, very high discount rates (interest rates) may reverse the conclusion. For example, if the safety key ratio is 1.5, self-rated savings exceed self-insured savings for discount rates up to and including 15 percent; the reverse is true for discount rates above 15 percent; if the key ratio is 2.0, the break-even discount rate is an unlikely 27 percent.

expenses—including a share of overhead—into each claim. By contrast, self-insureds will consider the marginal costs of an additional claim, without fixed overhead.

The faster that benefits and utilization are expected to grow, the greater the manual rate will be; hence, the greater the key ratio and the resulting prevention savings. Table 5.4 illustrates the current key ratios for selected industries in several states. Periods of significant benefit increases (like the 1970s) enhance safety incentives for two reasons. First, benefit increases directly increase the cost of injuries. Second, the safety key ratio is increased. When benefits and utilization begin to taper off, the key ratios will decline.[13]

This discussion suggests that, even ignoring insurer expense loadings, insurers may reward firms with more than a dollar premium savings for each dollar of the cost of claims prevented—on its face a curious result. Two questions arise: Why would insurance companies choose to do business this way? Why cannot competitive pressures force them to behave differently?

Recall that workers' compensation insurance rates have been set by regulation, and all insurers in a state charge the same rate.[14] This has historically been true, although the future may see regulation playing a smaller role in workers' compensation rate setting in many states. The approved rate-making conventions establish the procedures for computing manual rates, expected loss rates, trend factors, experience-rating formulas, and the like, for each state.

Insurance companies choose to reward a dollar of loss prevention with more than a dollar of premium savings because this is the way regulation has historically produced safety incentives in workers' compensation. Does that mean that they pay out more than they take in? No! Firms with greater than expected losses are penalized with premium increases that exceed the additional losses. This world is quite symmetric. In a perfectly regulated environment, as long as the rewards for prevention and the penalties for claims are equal, the world is in actuarial balance.

---

13. It is logically true that periods of significant benefit declines could drop the key ratio below the figures suggested in table 5.2.

14. Price competition may occur through a variety of discount devices, including formally filed deviations from the approved rates, phased payment plans, schedule rating, and the payment of ex post dividends; nonprice competition may occur through the provision of various services bundled into the insurance package—loss prevention and claims adjustment services are the most notable.

Why do not competitive pressures drive the rewards and penalties close to a dollar-for-dollar match between additional losses and
premiums? They might well do so if rates were not regulated or if
they were very imperfectly regulated. Moreover, as changing market
conditions cause actual pricing to depart from the regulated prices
through a variety of discount devices—rate deviations, schedule rating, dividends, and so on—the prevention incentives are reduced
proportionally. *There is one very important exception, however—competitive
price adjustments that use sliding-scale dividends.*

Since the amount of these dividends is tied directly to the safety
record of the insured, market conditions that dictate larger discounts
will actually enhance experience-rated prevention incentives by creating a pool of funds for discounts that is distributed according to
the insured's safety record.

Conventional View Revisited

With this as background, we reexamine the three commonly accepted
propositions about workers' compensation incentives.

Insured versus Self-Insured Incentives   The first proposition is that
self-insureds have the greatest savings from prevention and that insurance only dilutes these incentives. This belief has led to the search
for ways to enhance insured incentives, like the imposition of mandatory deductibles. We see, instead, in figure 5.1, that experience-
rated incentives may be substantially greater than self-insured incentives in medium- and large-size firms. In our example—for an insured
Georgia machine tool manufacturer with more than 125 employees—
prevention incentives exceed self-insured incentives by up to 50 percent for larger firms. The difference arises from an often ignored
feature of the experience-rating formulas that is most directly seen
and understood in the context of the self-rated firm. For this firm,
the savings from preventing some given loss (A) can be expressed as:

$$S = A \times \frac{MR}{ELR},$$

where MR is the manual or class insurance rate and ELR is the class-
expected loss rate.

This ratio will vary over time and among states, but it currently

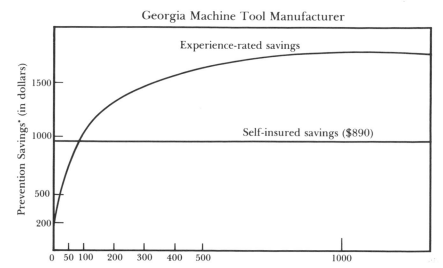

Figure 5.1
Experience Rating May Provide Greater Incentives than
Self-Insurance.

ranges from approximately two to three.[15] Thus, the actual dollar
savings in future premiums from preventing a loss *A* will be two or
three times *A*. Under the experience-rating procedures, one-third of
these savings occurs in each of three future years. Thus, the present
value of these savings taken from the point of view of the firm con-
templating prevention in the current period is approximately 1.6 to
2.4 times *A*.[16] By comparison, a self-insured saves 1.1 times the loss.[17]
In fact, the self-rated firm has the maximum prevention incentive.

We see that experience-rated incentives may well exceed self-
insured incentives by a substantial margin. The relationship of ex-

---

15. For further explanation of why the manual rate exceeds the expected loss
rate, see Victor (1983); see also NCCI Booklet, "An Indepth View of Experience Rating."
16. Assuming an 8 percent interest rate.
17. We assume that the loss adjustment expenses for an additional loss, ignoring
overhead, are 10 percent of the loss. We also assume that the claim accrues and is paid
completely in the same year. Otherwise, the loss development factors should be included
in addition. While these may vary widely from claim to claim, state to state, and class
to class, a ball park figure would be 15 percent (McAuley 1982).

perience-rated versus self-insured incentives depends upon the firm's size. For small firms, the firm's own experience is less credible and its premium is less sensitive to changes in its own experience. For a Georgia machine tool manufacturer, as illustrated in figure 5.1, experience-rated incentives exceed self-insured incentives for firms with more than 125 employees; but for firms with fewer employees, self-insured incentives are larger. (Of course, few firms with less than 125 employees self-insure.)

This relationship also differs according to the hazardousness of the industry. For more hazardous industries, the firm's experience is more credible for smaller and smaller firms, as seen in figure 5.2. In a very hazardous industry, like sawmills, experience-rated incentives will exceed self-insured incentives for firms with thirty or more employees; but in a much safer industry, like electronics, this point is reached at 200 employees. This suggests that generalizations are not easily made, but that the commonly accepted proposition that self-

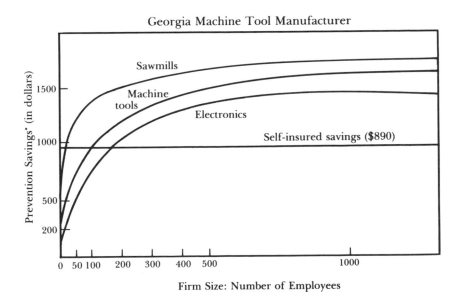

*For preventing a typical temporary total disability claim ($890).

Figure 5.2
Experience Rating May Provide Greater Incentives than Self-Insurance: Especially in High-Hazard Industries.

insureds have maximum incentives is not true for large firms, or even for relatively small firms in hazardous industries.

Adequacy of Prevention Incentives   Now we look at the second proposition: that workers' compensation incentives are inadequate. Of course, judgments about adequacy will vary. Reasonable people can and do disagree about what the appropriate standard should be. For illustrative purposes, we take one of the most commonly used standards for adequacy—that of economic efficiency.

Incentives are adequate under this standard when they impose the full costs of an injury upon the party who is in the best position to prevent the injury—where costs are both economic and noneconomic (e.g., pain and suffering). The workers' compensation system, through experience rating in large firms and even medium-size firms, imposes at least the full economic loss upon the employer, and sometimes more.[18] As shown in figure 5.3, if the noneconomic losses are up to 25 percent of the full economic loss, then the workers' compensation system will, through experience rating, provide adequate incentives.[19] Thus, we see that the workers' compensation system incentives are not necessarily inadequate.

Benefit Increases and Prevention Incentives   Finally, we look at the third proposition: that increasing workers' compensation benefits will generally increase employer incentives to take precautions in the workplace. This is a widely accepted view, although the literature has recently produced several examples of where this is not true (Viscusi 1980a). We offer one additional example here. Let us define the total employer prevention incentive as workers' compensation costs saved plus the portion of the compensating wage differential that the employer would save by undertaking prevention.[20] The compensating wage differential is an amount that the employer must pay the employee in return for the employee assuming some risk in the work-

---

18. This is true for the more frequent smaller loss, and for workers who are paid at or below the wage associated with the maximum wage loss benefit. For larger losses, the proportion of the total economic loss imposed on the employer falls. This is also true as employee wage levels rise above that maximum level.

19. This figure (25 percent) will vary from industry to industry, state to state, year to year, and injury to injury.

20. Of course, the total prevention incentive includes much more (e.g., downtime, damage to equipment, and so on).

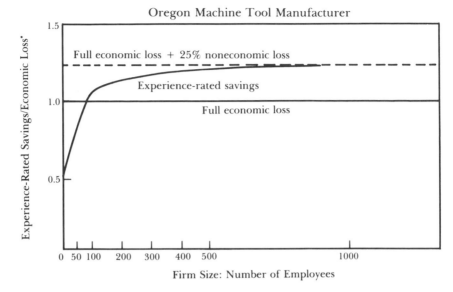

*Loss: Four-week temporary total disability; $450 medical.

Figure 5.3
Workers' Compensation Incentives Not Necessarily Inadequate.

place. In fact, the compensating wage differential is related to the uncompensated risk that the employee faces, not the total risk.

Thus, increasing workers' compensation benefits has two opposing effects: it increases the compensation costs imposed on the employer, but, it also reduces the uncompensated risk facing workers; hence, the compensating wage differential. For self-insured firms, the effects are exactly offsetting: higher benefits increase incentives by the same amount that they reduce the compensating differential component. From the firm's point of view, there is no net change in the safety incentives. By contrast, for self-rated firms, the increased workers' compensation benefits lead to more than proportional increases in safety incentives through experience rating. As we have seen, in present value terms, a one dollar benefit increase may yield an increase in incentives that is as much as two and a half times greater. From the worker's point of view, a one dollar benefit increase is a one dollar decrease in uncompensated risk, with the consequent reduction in the compensating wage differential. But this class-rated firm receives no safety incentives from experience rating. Thus, increasing workers' compensation benefits leads to a net reduction in prevention incentives.

The foregoing analysis suggests that experience rating may in fact provide greater incentives than self-insurance, especially for larger firms or small- and medium-size firms in more hazardous industries; in many cases, workers' compensation prevention incentives may be more than adequate—at least when judged by an economic efficiency standard; and increasing workers' compensation benefits may not increase employers safety incentives, especially for class-rated firms or self-insureds.

Other Uses of the Model

The simulation model that we used to generate the foregoing results has a number of other uses that may be of interest to policy makers, researchers, and insurance loss control professionals. First, as we have seen, it may be useful in assessing the adequacy of workers' compensation incentives. If one were to specify the adequacy standard that one thought appropriate, the simulation model could be used to characterize what the existing workers' compensation incentives are through the experience-rating mechanism and provide a basis of comparison and evaluation.[21]

Second, the simulation model, in providing these characterizations, can provide a basis for improved empirical research on workers' compensation and safety. To date, econometric attempts to characterize the effects of workers' compensation financial incentives on injury rates have largely failed because of the difficulty of properly measuring the workers' compensation incentives. The simulation model provides a vehicle for characterizing them appropriately.

Third, the simulation model may provide loss control professionals with a convenient means for bringing the true financial incentive for safety to the attention of employers. As such, it may prove useful for raising the safety consciousness of employers.

And finally, the simulation model may be most valuable for evaluating the consequences of a variety of reform proposals that

---

21. We have also constructed a simulation model for retrospective rating and prevention incentives that can be used in similar analyses. See Victor (1983).

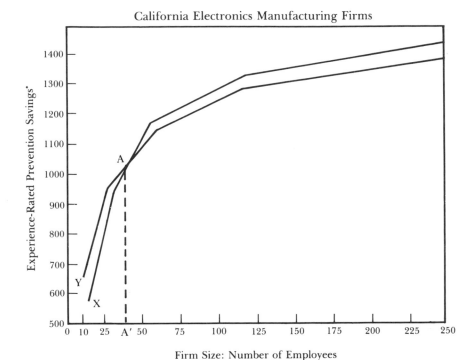

Figure 5.4
Mandating Deductibles May Reduce Safety Incentives.

have arisen either to enhance the safety incentives in the workers' compensation system or to enhance competition in the workers' compensation insurance market. For example, one proposal that has been advanced calls for mandating deductibles in the belief that this would increase the safety incentives in the workers' compensation system. As figure 5.4 shows, this change may lead to a net reduction in safety.

Line X indicates the safety incentives for California electronics manufacturing firms, before an introduction of a deductible. Line Y depicts the incentives with a $100 deductible. For firms with fewer than forty employees (point A), the incentives are increased since the firms now bear the full cost of that first $100. But for larger firms (and even medium-size firms), the introduction of a $100 deductible yields a net loss in the safety incentives because their experience is sufficiently credible that incurrence of a $100 loss previously raised the present value of future premiums by at least $100. The model demonstrates that the imposition of a deductible will not unambiguously increase safety incentives.

TABLE 5.1
Illustrative Primary and Excess Loss Values

Loss	Primary Loss	Excess Loss	Fraction in Primary Loss
1,000	1,000	0	1.00
2,000	2,000	0	1.00
3,000	2,727	73	0.91
5,000	3,846	1,154	0.77
10,000	5,555	4,445	0.56
25,000	7,576	17,424	0.30
50,000	8,621	41,379	0.17

TABLE 5.2
Illustrative Values of *W*

Total Expected Losses	Georgia	Oregon	North Carolina
15,000	0.00	0.00	0.00
50,000	0.06	0.02	0.04
100,000	0.19	0.06	0.13
250,000	0.56	0.17	0.39
500,000	1.00	0.35	0.83
1,000,000	1.00	0.73	1.00

TABLE 5.3
Expense Loadings and Safety Key Ratios

Expense Loading	Safety Key Ratio
0.30	1.43
0.33	1.50
0.40	1.67

TABLE 5.4
Illustrative Safety Key Ratios, 1979

State	Sawmill	Machine Tools	Electronics
California	2.14	2.12	2.11
Georgia	2.96	2.82	2.74
Mississippi	3.18	1.91	2.03
North Carolina	2.60	2.54	2.54
Oregon	2.75	2.66	2.66

6 · MINIMUM WEEKLY WORKERS' COMPENSATION BENEFITS

C. Arthur Williams, Jr.

All states except Arizona and Nevada have statutes that prescribe at least one type of minimum weekly benefits in their workers' compensation laws. Yet this feature of workers' compensation has received surprisingly little attention in the literature. In this chapter I will describe and analyze current minimum weekly workers' compensation benefits in the fifty states and the District of Columbia; examine the rationales that have been presented for such benefits; trace historical changes in minimum weekly benefits; and compare these benefits with the minimum weekly benefits provided in two other major social insurance programs: unemployment insurance and Old Age, Survivors and Disability Insurance.

Characterisics of Current Minimum Weekly Benefits

Workers' compensation benefits can be classified as medical expense benefits, disability benefits, and death benefits. The disability benefits may in turn be divided into total and partial disability benefits. In most states minimum weekly benefits are a feature of total disability benefits, partial disability benefits, and death benefits.

Total Disability Benefits   A typical workers' compensation statute sets the weekly cash benefit for a totally disabled worker at two-thirds of the worker's predisability earnings subject to a minimum and a maximum benefit. If the worker is temporarily disabled, he or she will receive this benefit either until the disability ends, or until a stated number of weeks have passed, whichever comes first. If the worker is judged to be permanently disabled, the benefit will continue until the disability ends. All but three states prescribe the same minimum weekly benefit for both temporary and permanent total disabilities.

Temporary Total Disability   All states except Rhode Island provide a minimum weekly temporary total disability benefit. Five of these states prescribe a minimum benefit, though not by statute. The statutory minimum benefits provided in the other forty-four states plus the District of Columbia vary greatly as to how the minimum benefits are determined and the dollar amount awarded. Table 6.1 summarizes these statutory provisions as of January 1, 1982, according to the method used to determine the minimum benefit.

　　Thirty of the forty-five jurisdictions with a statutorily prescribed minimum benefit expressed the benefit as a dollar amount. The other fifteen jurisdictions had a flexible minimum expressed as a percentage of the state average weekly wage (SAWW).

　　Twenty-three jurisdictions had a minimum benefit that permitted some workers to collect more than their actual wage loss. In most of these states, however, the minimum was so low that it affected few workers. Four of these twenty-three jurisdictions had a two-tier minimum that permitted workers with wages in excess of the lower minimum to collect at most only their actual wage loss. The other twenty-two jurisdictions never permitted the worker to collect more than the actual wage loss. One of these states, Oregon, limited the recovery to 90 percent of the actual wage loss.

　　Table 6.2 categorizes the forty-five jurisdictions specifying statutorily a minimum weekly benefit according to the dollar value of the benefit and the dollar value expressed as a percentage of the 1980 SAWW. (The 1980 SAWW is used as the reference point because the states that express the minimum weekly benefit as a percentage of the SAWW were using the 1980 SAWW as of January 1, 1982.) The jurisdictions are also subdivided according to whether they state the benefit as a percentage of the SAWW and whether they pay the actual wage, if less. The dollar values vary greatly. States that express the minimum as a percentage of the SAWW tend to prescribe higher minimum benefits.

Permanent Total Disability   All states except Rhode Island and Wyoming provide a minimum weekly permanent total disability benefit. As of January 1, 1982, these benefits were the same as the minimum weekly temporary disability benefits shown in table 6.1 for all states except Illinois and Massachusetts.

Partial Disability Benefits   Temporary partial disability benefits resemble temporary total disability benefits except that the disabled person typically receives two-thirds of the reduction in the worker's wage because of his or her partial disability. The minimum weekly benefits tend to be the same.

Most partial disability benefits, however, are permanent partial disability benefits. Permanent partial disability benefits in turn can be classified as scheduled or nonscheduled permanent partial disability benefits. To receive scheduled benefits the worker must have suffered a scheduled impairment such as the loss of use of an arm, the loss of use of a leg, the loss of sight in one eye, or a specified degree of disability because of a back ailment. The benefit, payable in a lump sum, is typically a weekly benefit dependent upon prior earnings multiplied by a specified number of weeks that varies with the nature of the impairment. The weekly benefit amount is typically two-thirds of a worker's predisability earnings, subject to a specified minimum and maximum.

Fewer jurisdictions provide minimum weekly partial disability benefits than those providing minimum weekly total disability benefits, and the minimums that are provided are frequently less liberal. As of January 1, 1982, all but five states had a minimum weekly scheduled permanent partial disability benefit. Nine of these states had a minimum benefit, though this minimum was not established by statute. Tables 6.3 and 6.4 summarize the minimum weekly scheduled permanent partial disability benefits in the other 37 jurisdictions in the same way that tables 6.1 and 6.2 summarize minimum temporary total disability benefits. Twenty-six of these 37 jurisdictions expressed the minimum as a dollar amount. The other 11 had minimums that were a specified percentage of the SAWW.

Nineteen jurisdictions permitted some workers to collect more than their actual wage loss. Only one of these jurisdictions had a two-tier minimum. The other 18 jurisdictions limited the worker's recovery to his or her actual wage loss.

A worker who is permanently partially disabled but not by a scheduled impairment receives a nonscheduled benefit. The weekly benefit is typically two-thirds of the wage loss (defined as wage after return to work less prior earnings) subject to a minimum and maximum amount. The benefit is payable until the worker no longer suffers a wage loss.

In most states, as of January 1, 1982, the minimum weekly unscheduled benefits were the same as the minimum scheduled benefits, but 9 states that had minimum weekly scheduled benefits had no minimum weekly unscheduled benefits. Consequently, in only 37 states was a minimum benefit paid for unscheduled permanent partial disabilities. Only 28 states prescribed such a minimum statutorily.

Death Benefits   If a worker dies because of a job-related injury or disease, his or her surviving spouse and children usually receive weekly benefits related to the worker's prior earnings. In about half the states the weekly benefit is 66.66 percent of the worker's prior earnings. In most of the other states the percentage is lower for a surviving spouse without children than for a surviving spouse with children. In both cases the weekly benefit is subject to minimum and maximum amounts. The most liberal states continue the benefits for the spouse for life or until remarriage. Children receive benefits until they are eighteen. Some states, however, terminate benefits after a specified number of weeks.

If no spouse survives the deceased, benefits may be payable to orphaned children. If no spouse or children survive the deceased, benefits may be payable to other dependent relatives. Only the benefits payable to surviving spouses with or without children will be discussed here.

As was true for permanent partial disability benefits, fewer states prescribed minimum weekly death benefits than minimum weekly total disability benefits. However, the minimums that are prescribed tend on average to be about the same.

As of January 1, 1982, 19 jurisdictions applied different minimums to death benefits than to total disability benefits, but in most cases the differences were small. All but 4 states had a minimum weekly death benefit. Six of these states provided a minimum benefit but not statutorily. Tables 6.5 and 6.6 summarize the minimum weekly death benefits in the other 41 jurisdictions in the same way that tables 6.1 and 6.2 summarize minimum weekly temporary disability benefits.

Twenty-six of these 41 jurisdictions prescribed a minimum dollar amount. The other 15 expressed the minimum as a percentage of the SAWW. Twenty-five jurisdictions did not reduce the minimum if the worker's wage was less. Only 16 paid the actual wage if less.

Summary Comparison   Table 6.7 summarizes the major characteristics of the minimum weekly benefits paid as of January 1, 1982 for temporary total disability, permanent total disability, scheduled permanent partial disability, and death cases.

Most states had minimum weekly benefits under all four categories. Minimum weekly permanent partial disability benefits were the least common. Under all four categories except death benefits, more than half the states with statutorily prescribed minimum benefits paid the actual wage if that amounted to less. The apparent reason for more liberal death benefits is that malingering is a major concern for disability but not death cases.

The average minimum benefit was about fifty-seven dollars for all benefit categories except permanent partial disability benefits. The upper end of the range was highest for death cases and lowest for permanent partial disability.

The average minimum benefit expressed as a percentage of the SAWW was about 21 percent for all four categories. The upper end of the range was highest for total disability and lowest for permanent partial disability.

States that had high minimum weekly temporary total disability benefits expressed as a percentage of their SAWW tended to have high minimum permanent partial disability and death benefits. Thirty-two states had minimums for all three categories of benefits.

The Spearman rank correlation coefficients for the three possible comparisons of ranking for these thirty-two states were as follows:

Temporary total disability, permanent partial disability   .915
Temporary total disability, death   .790
Permanent partial disability, death   .931

Only three states (California, Maryland, and North Dakota) changed their rankings by more than five places in the first comparison. Similarly only three states (Alaska, Maryland, and North Dakota) in the second comparison and only two states (Alaska and North Carolina) in the third comparison changed their rankings this much.

The Rationale for Minimum Weekly Benefits

Despite the fact that all states except Arizona and Nevada prescribe statutorily a minimum weekly benefit for at least one type of disability or death, the literature on workers' compensation sheds little light on the rationale for minimum weekly benefits.

The authors who discuss the rationale can be grouped roughly into three categories: the "sop" or token theorists; the "subsistence level" or "basic security" theorists; and those who question whether workers' compensation should provide a minimum weekly benefit at all. The token theorists tended to write in the 1920s and early 1930s, the subsistence level theorists in the late 1930s through the early 1950s, and the questioners in the 1970s.

The "Sop" or Token Theorists   The "sop" or token theory describes what its developers perceived to be actual behavior, not desired behavior. The sop theory is most closely associated with Rubinow, considered by many to be the father of social security in the United States. In *The Quest for Security*, Rubinow (1934, 99) listed three possible ways in which weekly disability benefits might be determined: equal and uniform, adjusted to need, and adjusted to the income loss. Because workers' compensation replaced a tort liability system, he noted, it was inevitable that workers' compensation benefits would be adjusted to the worker's pre-injury wage. Most early laws included a 50 percent wage replacement rate that Rubinow considered inadequate for all workers, especially for the lower wage groups. In his view even "the economical legislators and the even more economical employers could not help admitting" the dreadful plight of these lower paid workers. Consequently, as a sop to calm some protests, a minimum standard of compensation was introduced, usually five dollars a week and even as low as four dollars in some states (Rubinow 1934, 101). In other words, the minimum benefit was a sop or token exchange for too low a replacement ratio.[1]

Downey (1924, 35), who was the first to justify workers' compensation on the basis of least social cost, was, like Rubinow, a token theorist. Downey agreed that the worker's indemnity should be commensurate with the wage loss. Like Rubinow, however, he favored a much higher replacement rate than most early laws provided. Downey also saw no rational economic or ethical justification for a maximum weekly benefit. He did not pass judgment explicitly on whether workers' compensation should include a minimum benefit, but he summarized then current practices as follows: "The . . . minima are of no consequence, being usually fixed at the wage of the youngest child or the greenest apprentice" (Downey 1924, 57). In practice, therefore, he considered the minimum weekly benefit to be a token benefit set equal to the wage of the lowest paid worker.

The Subsistence Level or Basic Security Theorists   A different perspective is provided by Reede in his comprehensive analysis of the adequacy of workers' compensation. Reede (1947, 94) argued that the purpose of a minimum weekly benefit is to protect the disabled worker and his or her family against living at a lower standard than subsistence. In another section he described the purpose as protection from subjection to inhumanly low living standards (1947, 145). He noted with disapproval that in some states "the purpose of the minimum weekly wage is confused over the possibility of malingering, and the amount fixed is accordingly made subject to an actual wage provision." However, he noted that such provisional minimums are not objectionable if they are interpreted to mean the amount the worker would earn if at work full-time (1947, 94). Reede therefore argued that the purpose of the minimum benefit is maintenance of a subsistence standard of living; if, however, the worker's actual full-time wage were less than the benefit would be, the actual wage could be paid.

Some subsistence level theorists would never pay less than the subsistence level. For example, Millis and Montgomery (1938, 211)

---

1. Although Rubinow (1934) is the most explicit exponent of the sop theory as an explanation of actual behavior, his statements suggest that he personally favored a subsistence level minimum. For example, on p. 100 he states that workers' compensation fails in its primary social purpose unless it enables the worker and his or her dependents to live without physical or moral deterioration, undue suffering, and appeal to public or private charity.

observed that "the standards set have been influenced by the idea of maintenance. The granting of additional-benefits for dependents is thus explained. So are the maximum and minimum, in terms of so many dollars per week, rather than by the desire to maintain the standard of living, be it high or low, in the given case."[2]

Other observers have voiced similar concerns. For example, Armstrong (1932, 259) indirectly endorsed the subsistence level theory when she wrote that the "minima" of the various laws are still too small to prevent destitution. In an extensive analysis of the problems of workers' compensation Dawson (1940) noted that the location of the "floor" and the "ceiling" on benefits is of vital importance to workers, but he did not explain why a floor was otherwise justified. He did report that during the Depression of the 1930s some administrators put an absolute value on the minimum benefit at approximately a "subsistence" level (1940, 80). In their comprehensive study of workers' compensation, Somers and Somers (1954, 61) stated only that "the minimums which were once important and intended to give some basic security to the lowest-paid workers especially during periods of unemployment, have in many states lost their significance owing to rising wage levels." In her analysis of the decisions to be made in designing a social security program, Burns (1956) noted that the principle of relating benefits to wages has one serious disadvantage. The lowest benefits are paid "to those whose earnings are lowest and whose private resources for tiding over periods of nonearning are likely to be least" (1956, 41–42). Statutory minimum benefits have evolved as a common way of handling this problem.

The Questioners   More recently, some prominent workers' compensation scholars have questioned the rationale for minimum benefits. Three examples illustrate the line of reasoning behind their questioning.

In its 1972 report, the National Commission of State Workmen's Compensation Laws made over eighty recommendations for changes in state workers' compensation laws, nineteen of which it deemed essential. None of these recommendations mentioned minimum weekly benefits. The report emphasized, however, that the com-

---

2. For an argument that when the wages are very low there should be a minimum payment according to the number of dependents, see Van Doren (1918, 305).

mission did not recommend high minimum weekly benefits because it assumed that a family assistance program, or some other income maintenance program, would soon assure all families at least a subsistence income (National Commission 1972, 58). In the absence of such an income maintenance program, the commission acknowledged that a minimum benefit might be needed to avoid committing a low-wage disabled worker to welfare, a goal that the subsistence level theorists would applaud (1972, 37). However, the commission stated, "the basic insurance purpose of workers compensation suggests that the program should not be expected to remove low-wage workers from poverty if they are so unfortunate as to suffer a work-related injury or disease" (1972, 58).

In a research report submitted to the National Commission, Berkowitz (1973) argued that under the theory of workers' compensation, a worker should be compensated for only a portion of his or her wage loss. If the income lost is itself inadequate, nothing in the structure of workers' compensation can alter that situation. If society's objective is a minimum adequate income, that task should be assigned to a welfare program that bases benefits upon demonstrated need and is not limited to workers with job-related injuries or diseases (1973, 189–274, esp. 267–68).

However, Berkowitz concludes, "at extremely low wages, it may be justifiable, on some distributional grounds, to award the employee his actual wage" (1973, 268).

In a review of research conducted for the Interdepartmental Task Force on Workers' Compensation, Conley and Nobel (1979, 1:74) presented a case for eliminating the minimum weekly benefit. Minimum benefits, they argue, in effect require employers to subsidize welfare programs. If the calculated benefit is too low, the worker should apply for aid from a welfare program. Workers' compensation costs should internalize only the cost of work-related economic losses. Finally, eliminating the minimum benefit would remove a possibly important work disincentive.

Rationale Favored by the States   Workers' compensation laws of most states have demonstrated that of the three views on the rationale for a minimum weekly benefit, the token theory generally underlies state policy.

As stated previously, all states other than Arizona and Nevada prescribe statutorily a minimum weekly benefit for at least one type of workers' compensation benefit. Most states, therefore, share the view that workers' compensation should provide a minimum benefit. The subsistence level theory is not popular among the states. Tables 6.2, 6.4, and 6.6 show that only a few states provide a benefit that comes close to meeting a subsistence standard. For example, as of January 1, 1982, only three states (Minnesota, North Dakota, and Pennsylvania) had a minimum weekly temporary total disability benefit that equaled or exceeded the weekly earnings corresponding to the federal minimum wage. Only ten jurisdictions (District of Columbia, Idaho, Illinois, Minnesota, North Dakota, Ohio, Pennsylvania, South Dakota, Vermont, and West Virginia) had minimums for this benefit that equaled or exceeded half the federal minimum wage level standard. None had a minimum weekly benefit as high as the $162 1981 poverty level for a four-person family. Only ten provided a minimum that was as high as the $85 1981 poverty level for a single person under age sixty-five. Furthermore, eight of these ten states paid the actual wage if less than the minimum benefit.

Most states pay small minimum weekly benefits that are best explained by the token theory. Today, however, no state replaces less than 60 percent of a disabled worker's wage; all but a few pay two-thirds of the wage loss. Consequently, the argument Rubinow advanced for the sop or token theory is no longer valid.

The continuance of small minimum weekly benefits may merely reflect inertia on the part of these states to remove a benefit feature that is now outdated. An alternative explanation is that these states believe that no person suffering a job-related injury or disease should receive less than some token benefit. Because workers' compensation is the exclusive remedy of the employee against the employer, these states may reason that the worker should receive at least some small weekly amount (or the wage, if less) for the injury or disease itself.

Historical Development

Minimum weekly benefits have been a feature of most workers' compensation laws since these laws were first enacted. To illustrate how these minimums have changed over time, table 6.8 shows the minimum weekly temporary total disability benefits provided by the fifty states plus the District of Columbia in the original acts and as of July 1940, December 1968, and January 1982. The table expresses the minimum weekly benefit in dollars and, except for the original act, as a percentage of the SAWW. Table 6.9 summarizes some key characteristics of the minimum benefits in 1940, 1968, and 1982.

The number of states with specified minimums has changed only slightly over time: 45 in their original acts, 48 in 1940, 50 in 1968, and 45 in 1982.[3] However, whereas in 1982 15 states set the minimum as a percentage of the SAWW, only 2 states did so in 1968 and none in 1940. About one-half of the states have always paid the actual wage if less (including the states with a lower tier): 26/45 in 1982, 24/50 in 1968, and 25/50 in 1940.

In 1940 the average minimum expressed as a percentage of the SAWW was 31 percent, but by 1968 the average had declined to 18 percent. In 1982 the average was 21 percent—higher than in 1968, but lower than in 1940.

For many states the changes in the minimum benefit from 1940 to 1982 were dramatic. Five states increased their minimum by at least 15 percentage points during that time span: Idaho, Minnesota, North Dakota, South Dakota, and Vermont. Thirteen states decreased their minimum by at least 20 percentage points: Arkansas, Connecticut, Florida, Hawaii, Massachusetts, New Hampshire, New Mexico, North Carolina, Oklahoma, South Carolina, Tennessee, Texas, and Wyoming.

From 1940 to 1968 only four states increased their minimums as a percentage of the SAWW. In the remaining states the minimum benefit was reduced. From 1968 to 1982, however, twenty-two states increased their minimums. Most of the other states reduced their minimums, though in general only by a few percentage points.

The five states with the highest minimums, expressed as a percentage of the SAWW in 1940, 1968, and 1982, are as follows:

1940: Wyoming (49%); Hawaii (47%); New Mexico (45%); Arkansas (44%); North Carolina (44%).

---

3. The decline from fifty to forty-five in 1982 may be misleading. States in which a minimum was payable but not statutorily prescribed in 1982 were listed in 1968 as having a minimum. Because Alaska and Mississippi had no workers' compensation acts in 1940, these two states are not listed under either the original act or the 1940 column. Both states included a minimum benefit in their original acts.

1968: Washington (33%); Wyoming (33%); Pennsylvania (30%); Nebraska (29%); Oregon (26%); Vermont (26%).

1982: North Dakota (60%); Minnesota (50%); Pennsylvania (50%); South Dakota (50%); Vermont (50%).

No state appears in all three categories; only Pennsylvania, Vermont, and Wyoming appear in two of the three categories. The 1940 and 1968 rankings of the 1982 top five were as follows:

	1940	*1968*
North Dakota	28.5	24.0
Minnesota	15.5	27.5
Pennsylvania	6.0	3.0
South Dakota	13.0	8.0
Vermont	15.5	5.5

Washington and Wyoming experienced the greatest change in philosophy since 1940. In 1940 these two states paid a workers' compensation benefit that varied only with the number of dependents rather than with the worker's wage. For a given number of dependents, therefore, the minimum benefit and maximum benefit were the same. By 1968 Wyoming had adopted the more standard percentage replacement approach, but Washington did not do so until shortly thereafter.

Spearman rank correlation coefficients for the three possible comparisons of rankings also indicate significant shifts in these rankings among the years. The coefficients for these three rankings are as follows:

1940, 1968	.141
1940, 1982	.095
1968, 1982	.416

Proportion of Workers Affected by Minimum Benefits

An important factor affecting a state's decision to include a minimum benefit and the size of that benefit is its cost. This cost in turn depends upon the proportion of workers affected. According to the 1973 Standard Wage Distribution Table compiled by the National Council on Compensation Insurance, the proportion of disabled workers with wages below selected percentages of the SAWW is as follows:[4]

Percentage of SAWW or Less	Proportion of Disabled Workers
20%	1.44%
30	2.91
40	4.73
50	8.22
60	15.33
70	25.96
80	37.51
90	48.23
100	58.40

Assuming a two-thirds replacement ratio, a 20 percent minimum benefit would affect workers with wages equal to 30 percent or less of the SAWW. A 60 percent minimum would affect workers with wages equal to 90 percent of the SAWW.

Comparing these percentages with table 6.2 indicates that the token benefits provided by most states affect very few workers and have little impact on costs. On the other hand, the more generous 50 to 60 percent minimums affect many more workers and have fairly significant cost consequences.

Minimum Benefits in Two Other Social Insurance Programs

The final question to be explored in this paper is whether the philosophy and practice of minimum weekly or monthly benefits in unemployment insurance and Old Age, Survivors, and Disability Insurance shed any light on the rationale for a minimum weekly workers' compensation benefit.

Unemployment Insurance   All states prescribe statutorily minimum weekly unemployment insurance benefits. Table 6.10 compares the 1982 state minimum weekly unemployment insurance and workers'

---

4. The percentage of workers affected by the minimum weekly benefit will be somewhat less than the proportions shown in the text because tables 6.2, 6.4, and 6.6 express the minimum weekly benefit as a percentage of a prior year's SAWW.

compensation temporary disability benefits using the same format as tables 6.7 and 6.9.

The major findings are as follows:

More states prescribe statutorily minimum weekly unemployment insurance benefits than minimum weekly workers' compensation benefits.

Minimum weekly unemployment insurance benefits are much less likely to be prescribed as a percentage of the SAWW.

Minimum weekly unemployment insurance benefits are never reduced if the actual wage is less. On the other hand, to qualify for any unemployment insurance benefits, a worker must have earned a specified amount of wages or worked for a certain period of time within some base period preceding the unemployment.

Minimum weekly unemployment insurance benefits tend to be much smaller than minimum weekly workers' compensation benefits.

No apparent relationship exists between states that pay relatively high minimum weekly unemployment insurance benefits and those that pay relatively high minimum weekly workers' compensation benefits. The Spearman rank correlation coefficient for the forty-four states that prescribe statutorily both types of minimums is only .183 for rankings by dollar amounts and .121 for rankings by percentage of SAWW.

The literature on unemployment insurance is almost silent on the reason for including a minimum weekly benefit. In their comprehensive study of unemployment insurance Haber and Murray (1966, 111, 174) reported that although the Committee on Economic Security recommended no minimum weekly benefit, practically all the states included such a minimum in their original laws. They also noted that the "minimum amount has never received much attention in discussions of what benefits should be."

State practices, however, suggest that no state has adopted the subsistence level or basic security argument. The small state minimums suggest that the token theory underlies most state policies. Another possible explanation is that since the original unemployment insurance systems were patterned so closely on existing workers' compensation programs, the minimum weekly benefit feature was incorporated without much thought about its rationale. Two reasons the unemployment insurance minimums may generally be smaller than the workers' compensation minimums are that workers do not surrender any tort liability rights against their employers to secure unemployment insurance and unemployed workers who are not disabled by a job-related injury or disease have not experienced any disability-related pain and suffering or impairment.

Old Age, Survivors, and Disability Insurance   The nation's largest social insurance system—Old Age, Survivors, and Disability Insurance (OASDI)—has provided minimum monthly benefits since the Social Security Act of 1935 became effective. In recent years, until the extremely important 1981 amendments, OASDI provided regular minimum benefits and special minimum benefits. The regular minimum benefit was the smallest monthly amount that would be paid to workers as a retirement benefit or, at a younger age, as a disability benefit. If a worker died prior to retirement at age sixty-five, the minimum monthly benefits paid to survivors were expressed as a percentage of this regular minimum. The special minimum benefit was reserved for individuals with many years of service in covered employment at a low-earnings level. Although much higher than the regular minimum benefit, the special minimum level was not sufficient to keep the worker out of poverty.

According to Robert J. Myers (1981), for many years chief actuary of the Social Security Administration, the regular minimum benefit was originally introduced for administrative reasons, namely, to facilitate payments in low monthly benefit cases. Later, "it was viewed as a payment applicable to low-income workers and hence, according to social insurance principles, should be raised proportionately more than other benefit amounts" (Myers 1981, 185–86). More recently, it became apparent that many of the persons receiving this regular minimum benefit were not low-income workers. Instead, most recipients had spent only a small portion of their careers in covered employment. The rest of the time they had spent in other employments, which sometimes provided them with a generous pension, or had been unemployed. Support for a minimum payment that would benefit these persons as well as low-income workers gradually eroded.[5]

---

5. See, for example, *Reports of the 1979 Advisory Council on Social Security* (1979, 66).

In 1977, the minimum initial monthly award was frozen at $122; 1981 amendments terminated the regular minimum except for existing beneficiaries. The arguments were basically as follows: first, persons who did not rely solely on covered earnings for support during their working lives should not expect OASDI benefits to be their sole support in retirement; second, the regular minimum benefit was in many cases inconsistent with the generally accepted principle that benefits should be related to wages; third, public assistance programs such as Supplementary Security Income are a more appropriate way to provide a reasonable floor of protection for those persons who do not spend most of their working lifetime working full-time in covered employment (Williams 1982, 87–88).

The special minimum benefit, however, continues. Few question such a minimum. One reason may be that under the present provisions most eligible beneficiaries find that their regular benefits exceed the special minimum. However, the recent (1979) Advisory Council on Social Security suggested raising the special minimum benefit amount to the poverty level. Others believe the present special minimum benefit is already too generous. In any event the special minimum only applies to retirement benefits. OASDI no longer provides a minimum monthly disability benefit.

Conclusion

Minimum weekly benefits are an established feature of workers' compensation. Most states included minimum weekly benefits in their original laws. Today all but two states prescribe statutorily such minimums for at least one type of death or disability benefit.

Despite the almost unanimous endorsement in practice of minimum weekly benefits, the rationale for such a floor of protection is not clear. Two rationales have been suggested in the literature. According to the subsistence level or basic security theory, as a social insurance program workers' compensation should provide a minimum weekly benefit that allows a disabled worker and his or her dependents or the dependents of a deceased worker to maintain at least a subsistence standard of living. The pure form of this theory would pay this minimum amount even if the worker's earnings prior to disability or death were less than the minimum; a modified form would pay the actual wage if less.

According to the token theory, minimum benefits were introduced in the early days of workers' compensation as a sop to calm protests against some fundamental deficiencies in other early features of workers' compensation, particularly a low (50 percent) replacement rate. Although the features that originally generated these sop or token benfits have been improved, one can argue that benefits introduced as a sop remain because of a reluctance to remove benefits once they become an established feature of the system. An alternative interpretation of token benefits, not found in the literature, is that, because workers' compensation is the exclusive remedy of the employee against the employer, a disabled worker or deceased worker's family should be entitled to some minimum amount as compensation for such nonwage losses as impairments, pain and suffering, loss of household services, and limitations in personal activities. To prevent malingering, modified forms of these two interpretations of the token theory would accept payment of the actual wage, if that were less.

The subsistence level theory is the most thoroughly developed rationale in the literature, but even ardent supporters of this rationale spend little space developing their argument. A few states have minimums that are consistent with this theory, but most states pay small minimum benefits that are more aptly explained by the token theory.

States tend to be consistent in their minimum benefit philosophy across types of workers' compensation benefits, but there are some notable exceptions. Over time the states have not been consistent, with many states changing dramatically the relative generosity of their actions. If a philosophy guides their action, this philosophy must be changing over time.

Unemployment insurance and Old Age, Survivors, and Disability Insurance place much less emphasis on minimum benefits than does workers' compensation. Minimum weekly unemployment insurance benefits appear to have been copied initially from workers' compensation; however, they are generally much smaller than a state's minimum weekly workers' compensation benefit, and to be covered a worker must generally have earned at least a certain dollar amount during a base period. Until 1981, OASDI did pay disabled workers or the dependents of deceased workers a minimum monthly benefit, but that minimum was gradually being reduced in real dollars and in 1981 was discontinued for new beneficiaries. On the other hand, workers' compensation differs from these programs in one important respect that may explain the difference in emphasis on minimum benefits. Under workers' compensation, workers give up their right to sue employers under the tort liability system for losses not covered by workers' compensation benefits.

Minimum weekly workers' compensation benefits are thus subject to value judgments that vary among states and over time. The most common judgment at present apparently is that the law should include a small minimum benefit, which is consistent with the token theory, not the subsistence theory. Some states may have retained their minimum weekly benefits merely because of inertia, but the changes in most states have been too large for inertia alone to explain. Many states that originally had small minimums consistent with the sop theory now rank among the most liberal states and vice versa. Probably the most likely rationale for a minimum benefit in most states is inertia, plus some recognition that, although workers' compensation is the worker's exclusive remedy against the employer, it does not cover all the losses incurred by the employee because of a job-related injury or disease. This explanation, of course, assigns lesser value to the additional losses incurred by those employees who receive more than the minimum benefits. As workers' compensation costs increase and benefit priorities are more carefully examined, minimum benefits may become a less important feature of the system. Some states with high minimums may decide to reduce them, but most states will probably continue to provide some minimum weekly benefit.

TABLE 6.1
How States Determine Minimum Weekly Total Disability Benefits
(as of January 1, 1982)

	No.	Total	State
% SAWW		15	
Specified amount	4		ID, KY, NJ, WV
Wage if less, but no less than lower stated % of wage	3		HI, MN, PA
Wage if less	8		AL, DE, DC, LA, ND, OH, VT, VA
Dollar amount		30	
Specified amount	15		AR, CA, CT, KS, ME, MS, MO, NC, SC, TN, TX, UT, WA, WI, WY
Wage if less, but no less than lower stated dollar amount	1		MA
Wage if less	13		AK, FL, GA, IL, IN, IA, MD, NB, NH, NM, NY, OK, SD
90% of wage if less	1		OR
Payable but not statutorily prescribed		5	AZ, CO, MI, MT, NV
None		1	RI
Total		51	

Source: U.S. Department of Labor (1982). Table 6.

Notes: Table 6.1 shows minimum weekly temporary total disability benefits. All but three states prescribed the same minimum for permanent total disability. Illinois set the minimum permanent total disability award at 50% of the SAWW ($151.17). The Massachusetts minimum was $40 or the worker's predisability wage if less; there was no lower $20 minimum. Wyoming had no minimum weekly permanent total disability benefit.

Six states (Connecticut, Idaho, Massachusetts, North Dakota, Utah, and Virginia) paid additional benefits for dependents. Oregon paid additional dependents' benefits for permanent but not temporary total disability. Washington did not usually pay additional benefits for dependents, but its minimum benefit was higher when there were dependents. Illinois resembled Washington, but only with respect to temporary total disability benefits.

TABLE 6.2
State Minimum Weekly Total Disability Benefits
(as of January 1, 1982)

Minimum Benefit	No.	States Using Specified Amount	States Using Wage If Less
Dollar Amount			
$140–49	2		MD*, PA*
130–39	1		MN*
120–29	1		DC**
110–19	1		VT*
100–09	3	ID*	IL, SD
90–99	2	WV*	OH
80–89	0		
70–79	0		
60–69	4		AL*, DE*, HI*, AK
50–59	7	KY*, NJ*	LA*, VA*, IN, MD, OR
40–49	7	CA, MO, UT, WA, WY	NB, MA
30–39	6	NC	IA, NH, NM, NY, OK
20–29	9	CT, KS, ME, MS, SC, TX, WI	FL, GA
10–19	2	AR, TN	
	(45 total)		
% 1980 SAWW			
60%	1		ND*
55–59	0		
50–54	4		MN*, PA*, SD, VT*
45–49	1	ID*	
40–44	0		
35–39	1		DC**
30–34	3	WV*	IL, OH*
25–29	3		AL*, HI*, VA*
20–24	5	KY*, NJ*	DE*, LA*, NB
15–19	8	CA, MO, UT	IN, MD, MS, NM, OR
10–14	13	KS, ME, MS, NC SC, WA, WY	AK, GA, IA, NH, NY, OK
5–9	6	AR, CT, TN, TX, WI	FL
	(45 total)		

Source: Derived from U.S. Department of Labor (1982). Table 7.

Notes: *States that specify a percentage. Other states specify a dollar amount.

**The District of Columbia's minimum is 50% of the national average weekly wage but only 39% of the district's average weekly wage.

TABLE 6.3

How States Determine Minimum Weekly Scheduled Permanent Partial Disability Benefits (as of January 1, 1982)

	No.	Total	State
% SAWW		11	
Specified amount	4		MI*, NJ, OH*, WV
Wage if less, but no less than lower stated % of wage	1		HI
Wage if less	6		AL, DE, DC, LA, VT, VA*
Dollar amount		26	
Specified amount	14		AR, CA, CT*, MS, MO, NC*, ND, OR*, RI*, SC*, TN, TX*, UT**, WI
Wage if less	12		AK, GA, IL**, IN, IA, MD, NB, NH, NM, NY, OK, SD
Payable but not statutorily prescribed		9	AZ, CO, KY, MA, ME, MN, MT, NV, WA
None		5	FL, ID, KS, PA, WY
Total		51	

Source: U.S. Department of Labor (1982). Table 8.

Notes: *Scheduled disabilities only.

    **Illinois and Utah increase the minimum benefit when there are dependents.

TABLE 6.4

State Minimum Weekly Scheduled Permanent Partial Disability Benefits
(as of January 1, 1982)

Minumim Benefit	No.	States Using Specified Amount	States Using Wage If Less
Dollar Amount			
$120–29	1		DC**
110–19	1		VT*
100–109	2	OR	SD
90–99	1	WV*	
80–89	2		MI*, IL
70–79	1	OH*	
60–69	4		AL*, AK, DE*, HI*
50–59	5	NJ*	IN, LA*, MD, VA*
40–49	4	MO, ND, UT	NB
30–39	8	CA, NC, RI	IA, NH, NM, NY, OK
20–29	6	CT, MS, SC, TX, WI	GA
10–19	2	AR, TN	
	(37 total)		
% 1980 SAWW			
50–59%	2		SD, VT*
45–49	0		
40–44	0		
35–39	2	OR	DC**
30–34	1	WV	
25–29	6	MI*, OH*	AL*, HI*, IL*, VA*
20–24	4	NJ*	DE*, LA*, NB
15–19	6	MO, ND, UT	IN, MD, NM
10–14	11	CA, MS, NC, RI, SC	AK*, GA, IA, NH, NY, OK
5–9	5	AR, CT, TN, TX, WI	
	(37 total)		

Source: Derived from U.S. Department of Labor (1982). Table 8.

Notes: *States that specify a percentage. Other states specify a dollar amount.

**The District of Columbia's minimum is 50% of the national average weekly wage but only 39% of the district's average weekly wage.

TABLE 6.5
How States Determine Minimum Weekly Death Benefits
(as of January 1, 1982)

	No.	Total	State
% *SAWW*		15	
Specified amount	8		IL, KY, MI, NJ, OH, PA, VT, WV
Wage if less, but no less than lower stated % of wage	1		HI
Wage if less	6		AL, DE, DC, LA, VT, VA
Dollar amount		26	
Specified amount	17		AR, CA, CO, CT, KS, ME, MS, MO, NC, ND, NY, SC, TN, TX, UT*, WA, WI
Wage if less	9		AK*, FL, GA, IN, IA, MD, NB, NH, SD
Payable but not statutorily prescribed		6	AZ, ID, MN, NM, NV, OR
None		4	MA, OK, RI, WY
Total		51	

Source: U.S. Department of Labor (1982). Table 12.

Note: *Alaska and Utah increase the minimum benefit when there are dependents.

TABLE 6.6
State Minimum Weekly Death Benefits
(as of January 1, 1982)

Minimum Benefit	No.	States Using Specified Amount	States Using Wage If Less
Dollar Amount			
$170–79	1	MI*	
160–69	0		
150–59	1	IL*	
140–49	2	OH*, PA*	
130–39	0		
120–29	2		DC**, MT*
110–19	1	VT*	
100–109	1		SD
90–99	1	WV	
80–89	0		
70–79	0		
60–69	4	CO	DE*, HI*, AK
50–59	6	KY*, NJ*	LA*, VA*, IN, MD
40–49	6	CA, MO, UT, WA	AL*, NB
30–39	4	NY, NC	IA, NH
20–29	9	CT, KS, ME, MS, SC, TX, WI	FL, GA
10–19	3	AR, ND, TN	
	(41 total)		
% 1980 SAWW			
50–57%	7	IL*, MI*, OH*, PA*, VT*	MT*, SD
45–49	0		
40–44	0		
35–39	1		DC**
30–34	1	WV*	
25–29	3		AL*, HI*, VA*
20–24	6	CO, KY*, NJ*	DE*, LA*, NB
15–19	5	CA, MO, UT	IN, MD
10–14	11	KS, ME, MS, NY, NC, SC, WA	AK, GA, IA, NH
5–9	6	AR, CT, TN, TX, WI	FL
1–4	1	ND	
	(41 total)		

Source: Derived from U.S. Department of Labor (1982). Table 12.

Notes: *States that specify a percentage. Other states specify a dollar amount.

**The District of Columbia's minimum is 50% of the national average weekly wage but only 39% of the district's average weekly wage.

States with no minimum weekly death benefits: MA, OK, WY, RI.

States in which minimum weekly death benefits not statutorily prescribed: AZ, ID, MN, NM, OR, NV.

TABLE 6.7
Some Key Characteristics of Minimum Weekly Benefits
(as of January 1, 1982)

	Temporary Total	Permanent Total	Permanent Partial	Death
None	1	2	5	4
Payable but not statutorily prescribed	5	5	9	6
Minimum weekly benefit	45	44	37	41
% of SAWW	15	16	11	15
Absolute	4	5	4	8
Actual wage if less	11	11	7	7
Dollar amount	30	28	26	26
Absolute	15	14	14	17
Actual wage if less	15	14	12	9
Dollar Amount				
Average	$56	$57	$51	$58
Range	$15–142	$15–151	$15–124	$10–170
% of SAWW				
Average	21%	22%	21%	21%
Range	6–60%	6–60%	6–39%	4–50%

Source: U.S. Department of Labor (1982). Table 12.

TABLE 6.8
Minimum Weekly Temporary Total Disability Benefits:
Original Act, 1940, 1968, and 1982

State	Dollar Amounts				Percentage of saww		
	Original Act	July 1940	December 1968	January 1982	July 1940	December 1968	January 1982
Alabama	$5.00*	$5.00*	$15.00*	$60.00ᵃ*	31%	15%	25.00%
Alaska	(no law)	(no law)	25.00*	65.00*	(no law)	14	14.00
Arizona	—	—	30.00	?	—	26	?
Arkansas	7.00	7.00	10.00	15.00	44	12	7.00
California	4.17	6.50	25.00	49.00	22	19	17.00
Colorado	5.00*	5.00	13.00–	?	21	12	?
Connecticut	5.00	7.00	20.00	20.00	27	15	7.00
Delaware	4.00*	5.00*	25.00*	64.94ᵃ*	18	14	22.22
Dist. of Col.	8.00*	8.00*	18.00*	124.18ᵃ*	32	15	39.00
Florida	4.00*	6.00*	8.00*	20.00*	33	8	8.00
Georgia	4.00*	4.00*	15.00*	25.00*	24	15	10.00
Hawaii	3.00	8.00	18.00*	63.00ᵃ**	47	17	25.00
Idaho	6.00*	6.00–8.00	20.00	108.90ᵃ	28	20	45.00
Illinois	5.00	7.50	31.50	100.90*	26	24	34.00
Indiana	5.50*	8.80*	21.00	50.00*	36	17	18.00
Iowa	5.00*	6.00*	18.00*	36.00*	27	17	14.00
Kansas	6.00	6.00	7.00	25.00	27	7	10.00
Kentucky	5.00	5.00	22.00ᵃ	50.87ᵃ*	25	21	20.00
Louisiana	3.00*	3.00*	12.50*	55.00ᵃ*	14	11	20.00
Maine	4.00	6.00	18.00	25.00	30	18	11.00
Maryland	5.00*	8.00*	25.00*	50.00*	36	23	19.00
Massachusetts	4.00	9.00**	20.00**	40.00**	35	18	15.00
Michigan	4.00	7.00	27.42	?	22	20	?
Minnesota	6.00*	8.00*	17.50	134.00ᵃ**	33	15	50.00
Mississippi	(no law)	(no law)	10.00	25.00	(no law)	11	12.00
Missouri	6.00*	6.00*	16.00*	40.00	25	14	15.00
Montana	6.00*	8.00	34.50	?	32	34	?
Nebraska	5.00*	6.00*	30.00*	49.00*	26	29	21.00
Nevada	4.62*	6.92*	—	?	25	—	?
New Hampshire	—	7.00	20.00*	30.00*	35	20	13.00
New Jersey	5.00*	10.00*	15.00	58.00ᵃ	37	12	20.00
New Mexico	5.00*	10.00*	24.00*	36.00*	45	23	15.00
New York	5.00*	8.00*	30.00*	30.00*	27	23	10.00
North Carolina	7.00	7.00	10.00	30.00	44	11	13.00
North Dakota	6.00*	6.00*	15.00	140.00ᵃ*	28	16	60.00
Ohio	5.00*	8.00*	25.00*	99.33ᵃ*	30	19	33.33
Oklahoma	6.00*	8.00	15.00*	30.00*	32	14	11.00
Oregon	***	6.98*	29.92*	50.00*	29	26	18.00
Pennsylvania	5.00*	9.00**	35.00**	142.00ᵃ**	39	30	50.00
Rhode Island	4.00	8.00	25.00	—	35	24	—
South Carolina	5.00	5.00	5.00	25.00	33	5	11.00
South Dakota	6.00	7.50*	22.00*	104.00*	34	24	50.00
Tennessee	5.00*	5.00*	15.00**	15.00	27	15	6.00
Texas	5.00	7.00	9.00	25.00	30	8	9.00
Utah	7.00	7.00*	25.00*	45.00	30	24	18.00
Vermont	3.00*	7.00	27.00ᵃ*	113.00ᵃ*	33	26	50.00
Virginia	5.00	6.00	14.00	57.75ᵃ*	30	14	25.00

TABLE 6.8 (continued)

State	Dollar Amounts				Percentage of SAWW		
	Original Act	July 1940	December 1968	January 1982	July 1940	December 1968	January 1982
Washington	4.62	8.08	42.69	42.69	31	33	14.00
West Virginia	4.00	8.00	24.00	92.09a	35	20	33.33
Wisconsin	—	7.35	8.75	20.00	27	7	8.00
Wyoming	3.46	11.54	33.46	43.39	49	33	14.00

Source: Original act and 1940 data, except for Alaska, Hawaii, Washington, Oregon, and Wyoming from Reede (1947). Alaska, Hawaii, Washington, Oregon, and Wyoming data provided by U.S. Department of Labor, Office of Workers' Compensation Programs. 1968 data from U.S. Department of Labor Wage and Labor Standards Administration (1969).

Notes: For 1982 data see table 6.1

? Payable but not statutorily prescribed.

a Expressed as percentage of SAWW.

* Actual wage if less.

** Actual wage if less but not less than lower tier.

*** Oregon's temporary disability benefit was originally 50.00% of the predisability earnings if the worker was single; 60.00% if married; and 66.66% if married with children. The minimum benefit was 60.00% of the predisability benefit which affected only single persons. Therefore, Oregon has been classified in this study as not including a minimum benefit in its original act.

TABLE 6.9
Some Key Characteristics of Minimum Weekly
Temporary Total Disability Benefits: 1940, 1968, and 1982

	1940	1968	1982
No law	2	0	0
None	1	1	1
Payable but not statutorily prescribed	0	0	5
Minimum weekly benefit	48	50	45
% of SAWW	0	2	15
Absolute	0	1	4
Actual wage if less	0	1	11
Dollar amount	48	48	30
Absolute	23	25	15
Actual wage if less	25	23	15
Dollar amount			
Average	$7	$20	$56
Range	$3–11.54	$5–42.69	$15–142
% of SAWW			
Average	31%	18%	21%
Range	14–49%	5–33%	6–60%

Source: U.S. Department of Labor (1982).

TABLE 6.10

Some Key Characteristics of Minimum Weekly Temporary Disability
Workers' Compensation Benefits and Minimum Weekly Unemployment
Insurance Benefits (as of January 1, 1982)

	Workers' Compensation	Unemployment Insurance
None	1	1
Payable but not statutorily prescribed	5	0
Minimum weekly benefit	45	50
% of SAWW	15	6
Absolute	4	6
Actual wage if less	11	0
Dollar amount	30	44
Absolute	15	44
Actual wage if less	15	0
Dollar amount		
Average	$56	$23
Range	$15–142	$5–45
% of SAWW		
Average	21%	9%
Range	6–60%	1–18%

Source: U.S. Department of Labor (1982).

7 · SPECIAL FUNDS IN WORKERS' COMPENSATION

Lloyd W. Larson and John F. Burton, Jr.

A special fund in workers' compensation is a fund used to pay cash benefits, medical care, rehabilitation services, or administrative expenses when a certain specified contingency occurs. When the contingency occurs, the special fund is used instead of or in addition to the normal financing mechanism for workers' compensation. The special fund is financed by contributions from more than one employer or private insurance carrier, or from general revenues, or from a combination of these sources; a special account maintained by an individual employer or private insurance carrier is not considered a special fund for purposes of this study.

In the discussion that follows, some reference is made to devices that are not technically funds, but that are closely analogous and employ similar techniques. For instance, exclusive state funds may use special or segregated accounts to accomplish the same purposes that special funds do in states with competitive state funds or with

This study is based in part on "Special Funds in Workers' Compensation," a report submitted in 1981 to the Employment Standards Administration of the U.S. Department of Labor. We appreciate the support of the Department of Labor. We also appreciate the comments on that report received from Jeannette Tomasini Gómez, Donald Prudhomme, William Johnson, Donald Ridzon, Donald Seagraves, Eric Oxfeld, George Hatch, Robert Landess, June Robinson, Granville Lee, and C. Arthur Williams, Jr. We accept responsibility for any remaining errors. Finally, we express our thanks to Nancy Voorheis for typing the various versions of the study.

only private carriers, and some of these accounts are treated as special funds.

Special funds operate like insurers, insofar as they accumulate reserves for future losses in accordance with sound insurance principles. However, thay may also utilize other techniques not ordinarily available to private insurance companies, such as compulsion and taxation. The fund mechanism has two facets: the pooling of financial resources by those who contribute to the fund, and the pooling of losses of those affected by the insured contingency. In order for the insurance mechanism to operate successfully, its financial structure must be such as to guarantee in the long run that the resources acquired shall be at least equal to the losses incurred.

Purposes of Special Funds

Starting with the establishment of a second-injury fund in New York in 1916, special funds have played an important role in helping to solve the problems that arise under the normal mechanism for financing the workers' compensation program. This normal mechanism relies on private or state insurance carriers or self-insuring employers to pay the major portion of the costs of the program. Although this method of financing is reasonably successful, experience has revealed several problems. For example, some employers do not secure the payment of compensation, either by failing to purchase insurance or by not complying with the legal requirements for self-insurance. Injured workers of such employers may receive no benefits or must overcome great practical difficulties to obtain benefits. A second problem involves insolvency of carriers or self-insurers, which can leave injured workers with no recourse. Another common problem results from inflation and gains in productivity. Workers whose benefits are frozen at a level determined by their wages at the date of injury will suffer a severe diminution in the real value of their benefits paid over an extended duration. A related problem occurs for carriers and employers when benefits are paid over long durations. Reserves for future benefit payments are established shortly after the date of injury and may prove insufficient if the period of disability is prolonged. The problem is aggravated if benefits are adjusted through time in response to inflation.

Similar problems of inadequate benefits or inadequate reserves or both may occur when there is a long latency period between the date of exposure to a toxic substance and the date a disease occurs or becomes disabling. The worker will suffer if benefits are related to wages at the date of exposure, while the carrier or employer may have insufficient reserves if wages immediately prior to the date of disability are used to establish benefits. In any case, carriers may have difficulties establishing appropriate reserves in cases with long latency periods since a carrier is generally liable for all benefits pertaining to exposure during a policy period, even when the disease resulting from that exposure occurs years or even decades later.

Catastrophic accidents or incidents pose another problem for the normal financing mechanism since the individual carrier or employer may suddenly face an amount of liability that far exceeds reserves. Another problem is posed by small or undesirable risks, which are unprofitable for private carriers and may therefore have difficulty obtaining insurance. A final problem worth cataloging is that insurers or employers may be reluctant to hire the handicapped under the normal financing mechanism because of a concern that another injury to such a worker will result in an expensive case, such as permanent total disability, for which the carrier or employer will be liable.

Several solutions have been attempted for these various problems associated with the normal financing mechanism in workers' compensation. Sometimes the solution is simply to evade responsibility for the problem within the workers' compensation program. Thus, when the potential liability for benefits appeared too great, one solution was to limit the duration or amount of benefits. In order to limit uncertainty about future liability, various statutory limitations were used to bar claims. For example, statutes of limitations requiring claims to be filed within a relatively short period after the date of exposure to a toxic substance precluded recovery when the disease did not occur until much later. Uncertainty about future liability was also reduced by use of compromise and release agreements that extinguished the employee's right to further benefits in exchange for a lump sum. The administrative problems of dealing with small employers sometimes were solved by exempting them from coverage by the program.

The preceding solutions to the problems of the financing mechanism are generally undesirable in our view, but other approaches are more salutary. States have developed a set of compliance checks and penalties to minimize the number of uninsured employers. Private carriers and self-insurers are audited to ensure that reserves are adequate. To cope with the problem of catastrophic or other unanticipated losses, carriers generally reinsure part of their risks or use other insurance devices to reduce their exposure. Similarly, self-insuring employers often purchase excess cover insurance to protect themselves against unanticipated heavy losses. The problem of employers considered undesirable risks being unable to purchase insurance is dealt with in most states by assigned risk plans or pools, which allocate the undesirable risks among the carriers providing insurance in the state.

This brief survey of the problems of the normal financing mechanism for workers' compensation and of some of the solutions provides the context for our examination of special funds.[1] There obviously are a variety of problems and a panoply of solutions that can compete with or complement the special funds approach. Special funds are used upon the occurrence of certain contingencies associated with the problems of the normal financing mechanism. (For example, a fund may assume responsibility for payment of benefits when there is a catastrophic accident, which causes problems for the carrier or employer because reserves are insufficient.) Some states have used a separate fund for each contingency; others have combined several uses or purposes within a single fund. In the discussion that follows, we are more interested in the purposes of the funds than in their designation; thus, if a state has a fund that deals with second injuries, increases in benefits for old cases, and special funding for a rehabilitation program, each purpose will be discussed under the heading for that purpose, rather than under the name of the fund.

Special funds have been created on a piecemeal, ad hoc, and often haphazard basis by different states. These funds reflect the complexities of the workers' compensation program as well as the program's need to draw lines of demarcation between occupational and nonoccupational injuries and illnesses, between short-term and

---

1. The problems of the normal financing mechanism and possible solutions are considered in more detail in Larson and Burton (1981, chap. 2).

long-term disabilities, and between individual employer liability and collective responsibility. The funds have been structured according to the unique history of each jurisdiction, and as a result there are variations among states in the purposes, financing, administration, and investment and control of funds.

The existing funds do not represent all the possible uses to which the special fund approach may be applied. This chapter first briefly surveys all the current uses of special funds, then more closely examines two types of funds (second-injury funds and benefit adjustment funds), and concludes by considering the possible extended use of special funds to help compensate work-related diseases.

Special Funds Currently in Use

The principal types of special funds may be classified as follows:

1. *Second- or subsequent-injury funds*—to remove the perceived disincentive to the hiring or reemployment of handicapped workers (54 funds).

2. *Benefit payment guarantee funds*—to ensure that benefits due are actually paid even if the employer is not insured (21 funds), or if the insurer (44 funds) or self-insurer (11 funds) becomes insolvent.

3. *Benefit adjustment funds for long-term beneficiaries*—to keep compensation benefits at least partly updated in long-term disability and survivorship cases so as to minimize the erosion brought about by rising living costs (18 funds).

4. *Rehabilitation funds*—to help provide funding of rehabilitation services and thereby restore injured workers to productive and gainful employment (17 funds).

5. *Funds for continuation of payments in long-term cases*—to pay cash benefits (4 funds) or medical benefits (4 funds) in long-term disability or death cases while limiting the liability of the individual employer to a fixed, maximum amount.

6. *Occupational disease funds*—to provide compensation to workers disabled by chronic diseases resulting from the employment, especially in long-latency cases where the responsible employer is difficult or impossible to locate or identify (7 funds).

In addition to the above, which are found in a considerable number of states, the following miscellaneous funds have been established in only a few jurisdictions:

1. *Reopened cases funds*—to make it possible to reopen old cases without requiring the individual carrier or employer to defend against claims where proof may be difficult to secure.

2. *State funds for public employees*—to centralize financing of claims against state and local government employers.

3. *Reimbursement funds*—to reimburse employers for payments if it later develops that the claims were not valid.

4. *Funds providing additional health benefits for children*—to increase the amount of benefits made to dependent surviving children.

5. *Independent medical examination funds*—to pay for independent medical examination of claimants in certain contested cases.

6. *Funds providing legal assistance to claimants*—to provide information and assistance to claimants about the act and claims procedures.

7. *Catastrophe funds*—to provide for limitation of employer liability in cases where several employees of the same employer are killed or permanently and totally disabled in one accident.

The special funds in operation in the various states as of 1980 are shown in table 7.1. The data in this table show a considerable range in the number of funds that each jurisdiction has. Excluding the three United States programs, the other fifty-two jurisdictions (including the District of Columbia and Puerto Rico) have a total of 192 funds, for an average of 3.7 funds per jurisdiction. Sixteen of these jurisdictions have only 2 funds (in all instances, a second-injury fund and an insolvent carriers fund), and fifteen jurisdictions have only 3 funds. At the other extreme are states that use a substantial number of funds, such as New York (10); Minnesota (8); the District of Columbia (7); and Arizona, Connecticut, Michigan, Oregon, Pennsylvania, Washington, and Wisconsin with 6 each.

Second-Injury Funds

All states have second-injury funds, sometimes called subsequent-injury funds. The funds are used to provide workers' compensation benefits to a person with a prior impairment who suffers one or more subsequent injuries. These funds are designed to eliminate discrimination against handicapped or previously impaired workers. The funds attempt to accomplish this by shifting to the fund some or all of the costs of providing such workers with benefits that would not have been incurred but for their preexisting impairments. For example, a one-armed man who is hired and then loses the other arm in a work-related injury would be totally disabled. Under normal principles of worker's compensation law, and in the absence of a second-injury fund, the employer would be liable for permanent total disability benefits, even though another worker who suffered the loss of one arm would be entitled only to permanent partial disability benefits. Because of this potential extra cost, an employer might hesitate to hire a handicapped worker. The second-injury fund removes at least part of the economic motivation for discriminating against such applicants by paying the difference between the cost of all of the consequences of the injury actually incurred and the cost of that injury had there been no prior disability.

The second-injury fund principle recognizes that the full cost of disability sustained by the previously handicapped person should be borne by the workers' compensation program but attempts to distribute equitably the burden by spreading the extra costs incurred as a result of the prior impairment rather than let them fall on the last employer. The funds thus attempt to reconcile in part the view that "the employer takes the worker as he finds him," with the notion that the employer should not have to shoulder the full burden of certain defined losses which ought to be more broadly distributed.

The drafters of early compensation law apparently did not fully recognize how the law might be used to discriminate against handicapped workers. Second-injury funds proved to be an important device to discourage such discrimination. They were not widespread at the start of World War II. That war served to encourage the establishment of second-injury funds, for it dramatized the need to protect the disabled war veterans who were returning to civilian life. The labor shortage created by the war afforded an opportunity for the handicapped to be employed and demonstrate that they can perform effectively. In July 1940, there were fourteen funds in existence; by 1945 there were thirty-four such funds or equivalent arrangements (Larson 1973). Now, as indicated, all jurisdictions have such funds, although many of them have limitations, as will be described.

Coverage of Funds   Generally speaking, these funds are designed to cover second injuries that have unusually severe consequences because of interactions of the new injuries with previous disabilities. The types of cases covered by second-injury funds vary widely from law to law. Funds limit their application by specifying the nature or extent of the prior and subsequent injuries, and the sequence and consequences of the two that are required before the fund becomes operative.

Requirements for the Prior Injury   Many states require that the prior injury be the loss by amputation of, or the loss of use of, a specific body part, e.g., an eye, arm, hand, leg, or foot. Thus, many kinds of impairments are excluded, including some of the most common industrial handicaps, such as cardiac conditions and herniated disks. Even such an obvious impairment as the loss of hearing in one ear would be excluded under such narrow coverage laws.

The broadest approach covers all previous permanent impairments. A state may clarify this broad application of its law by indicating that the previous incapacity may be a result of accident, disease, or congenital condition.

An intermediate approach to coverage of prior injuries can be achieved by covering a broad range of impairments but adding an additional requirement. For example, a few states require that the prior injury be registered with the compensation board or at least that the employer have prior knowledge of the handicap. This requirement is designed to avoid arguments over which prior injuries are covered. Several states that have a broad coverage of preexisting injuries caused by accident do not cover disease.

As an example of an intermediate approach, Ohio limits coverage to twenty-four specified kinds of previous conditions, including epilepsy, diabetes, cardiac disease, arthritis, multiple sclerosis, and psychoneurotic disability. In contrast, Alaska, under a generally broad second-injury provision, only requires that the previous disability be physical (rather than mental).

Requirements for the Subsequent Injury   Most states require that the subsequent injury also be the loss of use or loss by amputation of the specific body parts named above. Others more broadly require simply a second or subsequent injury. Some require that the second injury be of a permanent partial nature.

A few states require that the second injury be of a specified degree of severity. California requires 35 percent disability, while Wisconsin requires that the second injury be one producing a 200-week or more permanent disability. Both of these requirements also apply to the prior injury.

Requirements for the Combined Effect of the Prior and Subsequent Injury Most states require that the prior and subsequent injuries result in permanent total disability. This requirement of permanent and total disability considerably restricts the usefulness of the fund, for such disability is comparatively rare. There were only about four thousand cases of permanent and total disability in a recent year, according to insurance company statistics gathered by the National Council on Compensation Insurance, or about 0.3 percent of all disabling injury cases.[2] Some states require as a final result either permanent total disability or permanent partial disability greater than that which would have been produced by the second injury alone. For example, New York requires that the combined effects of both conditions must result in a permanent disability "materially and substantially greater than that which would have resulted from the subsequent injury or occupational disease alone." Somewhere in between are California, which requires a disability of 70 percent resulting from both injuries together, and Maryland, which has a 50 percent of total disability requirement for both injuries together.

Most funds only pay for some kind of permanent disability. Thus, under most laws, a second-injury combining with a previous injury to produce death would not be covered by the fund. Also excluded by many of the laws are reimbursements for medical and rehabilitation expenses.

Previous Recommendations for Coverage   The *Workmen's Compensation and Rehabilitation Law* published by the Council of State Governments in 1965 (sometimes called the Model Act) provides guidance for these aspects of coverage (Section 20). The prior injury includes any physical impairment, whether congenital or as a result of injury or disease, that constitutes an obstacle to employment or reemployment. The prior injury must be one of twenty-six listed conditions that include amputated limbs, a ruptured disk, and cardiac disease. In addition,

---

2. The data are on a fifth-report basis (i.e., 66 months after the policy's effective date) and are reported in Berkowitz and Burton (forthcoming), table 4.4.

under a general clause, any previous injury that is rated at 50 percent or more of total impairment is included. The employer must establish by written record that the employer had knowledge of the prior injury when the worker was hired (or that the employee was not subsequently fired when the employer first learned of the previous condition). The second injury can be of any type so long as the prior injury and the subsequent injury combine to produce a disability that is substantially greater than the disability that would have resulted from the second injury alone, or produces death that would not have resulted from the second injury alone. The Model Act provides relatively broad coverage: since a large number of prior conditions are covered, there is no limitation on the type of second injury, and the resulting disability is not confined to permanent total cases but also includes serious permanent partial and death cases.

The National Commission on State Workmen's Compensation Laws (1972) also recommended that each state establish a second-injury fund with broad coverage of preexisting impairments.[3] The commission offered a word of caution on the scope of coverage, however:

> It is possible also to make the list of prior impairments covered so broad that virtually every employee can be found, by intensive medical examination, to have a physical limitation which would be compensable by the fund. Since the second-injury funds are usually financed by general assessments against all employers, such broad coverage subverts the policy of allocating the cost of injuries and diseases to the firms primarily responsible (National Commission 1972, 84).

Support for second-injury funds with broad coverage has also been provided by the federal Interdepartmental Workers' Compensation Task Force (1977, 16) and the International Association of Industrial Accidents Boards and Commissions (1983, 22).[4]

Allocation of Liability between Employer and Fund   Most funds pay the difference between the compensation payable for the second injury if it had occurred alone and that resulting from the combined effects of the two injuries.

---

3. See recommendation R4.10, pp. 83–85.
4. See standard 10.

Because of the difficulty in ascertaining the amount attributable to the second injury in broad coverage states, a few states establish arbitrary limits for the employer's liability and charge the fund with liability for any balance. In Florida and New York, the fund pays any amount owing after the first 104 weeks of disability; South Carolina pays all compensation benefits after the first 78 weeks. The Oregon fund pays all costs of the resulting disability, with the employer being freed of all liability. Minnesota pays for any disability in excess of 52 weeks and any medical expenses beyond $2,000. Wisconsin pays for the greater of the two injuries, while New Mexico apportions judicially between fund and employer, after the latter pays for the first 8 weeks of disability. Obviously, there is disagreement among the states about the extent to which the employer's liability should be limited in second-injury situations. The Model Act of the Council of State Governments, in Section 20(a), provides for an allocation of the liability between the employer and the fund based on the New York provision.

Financing Methods   There is little uniformity in the approaches used to finance second-injury funds. The funds are financed by one or more of the following alternatives: (1) a specified charge against employers or carriers in death cases where there are not any dependents and sometimes in other death cases; (2) assessments that are a percentage of compensation premiums; (3) assessments that are a percentage of all or a specified type of compensation losses; (4) appropriations from general revenues; (5) fines; (6) premium taxes; (7) payments due but not paid to nonresident alien dependents; and (8) sums recovered from third parties. In the case of some exclusive state funds, two other methods that can be used are: (9) reserves set aside out of statutory surplus; and (10) amounts not expended from the maximum budget allotment. The approaches used by the various states are shown in table 7.2.

Many states have arbitrary cut-off and start-up points for contributions to the fund. For example, Delaware suspends payments to the fund when it reaches $85,000 and resumes payment when it falls below $35,000. The highest cut-off point is Maryland's $1,000,000 while the lowest is $35,000 in Mississippi.

On the surface, the financing provisions of many of the funds may not appear to be fair. It could be argued, for example, that it is unfair to saddle those employers with no-dependency death cases with the costs of the second-injury fund since it is likely that other employers were responsible for the benefits paid by the fund. A partial rebuttal to this argument is that any scheme closely linking the benefits and costs of second-injury funds would be inappropriate, as the very purpose of the fund is to spread the cost broadly rather than to allocate it to the source of injury. In other words, precise cost allocation to the employer responsible for benefits paid by the fund would defeat the purpose of the fund, since the employer would be likely to discriminate against handicapped workers if the burden of the fund were placed on him or her. However, even if there is a good reason not to closely link the benefits paid to a particular employer's workers with the payments made by that employer to support the fund, the use of arbitrary rules to allocate the costs of the fund still seems unjust. Equity seems to require broad spreading of cost among employers; and payments in the event of no-dependency death cases are not a likely device to do so. Other alternatives, such as a percentage of compensation premium or of losses paid, are more likely to provide equitable assessment of cost.

In addition to the equity problems arising from the use of financing rules that are dependent on the occurrence of unusual events, whether such approaches are actuarially sound is a serious question. As will be discussed, the no-dependency death case financing simply has not managed to produce an adequate level of funding.

Investments   As is the case with an insurance company, investment income constitutes an important source of financial resources for the funds. Most funds, however, are quite limited in their investment alternatives. As an example, Alabama's second-injury fund may invest only in obligations of the United States government or the state of Alabama. Even within this limited investment authority, the investment income of the Alabama fund has equaled almost 80 percent of benefit payments.

A common investment provision is found in the Iowa statute (Section 85–66), which permits investment of the second-injury fund's reserves in "securities which constitute legal investments for state funds under the law of this state." Among others with similar provisions are Florida, Idaho, Maryland, and Missouri.

In accordance with traditional governmental investment practices, the investment policy pursued by funds is usually restrictive.

They tend to be influenced by the Depression philosophy that has permeated many government investment operations. To the extent that this results in more limited investment income, the funds needlessly sacrifice income that could result in lower costs to the funds.

Administration   In Iowa, the state treasurer is the custodian of the fund, and this is the approach normally used in states. Occasionally another state official is named custodian, such as the state director of the budget or the commissioner of labor.

Payment from the funds is typically ordered by the compensation board or agency. Authority to pay may be vested in a specified person such as the director of industrial relations. Awards usually specify the amount that shall be paid weekly to the injured employee, the number of weeks' compensation to be paid by the employer, the date that payments from the fund shall begin, and, to the extent practicable, the length of time the payments shall continue.

The fund is usually represented by the attorney general or his or her designee in legal or administrative proceedings. One purpose of such representation is to defend the fund against improper or unwarranted claims. New York has a special committee to perform this function.

Extent to Which Second-Injury Funds Are Used   The activity of the state second-injury funds is set forth in table 7.3, showing the cash balance, benefits paid, payments into the fund, number of claimants receiving benefits, and new claims filed. Many of the funds are relatively inactive, as the table indicates, but a few are making substantial payments. New York, for instance, with its 104-week cut-off on the employer's liability, paid out approximately $21.1 million in fiscal year 1979. (The exact amount is difficult to determine because the fund is also used for certain other programs.)

Since the amount of money available depends in large measure on the method of financing, the choice of financing methods has a significant effect on the extent to which the fund will be used to encourage the employment of the handicapped. For example, inasmuch as fewer than 1 percent of all job-connected injuries result in death, comparatively little income accrues to the second-injury funds supported solely by payments in such cases, especially if the contributions are only made in no-dependency cases and are for small amounts, such as $1,000 per case. Those inadequately financed funds are utilized very sparingly, whether in the "broad coverage" or "narrow coverage" states. The reason is not difficult to establish. Where the financial base for a fund is constricted, as is almost certainly the case where no-dependency death payments are the sole source of support, and the coverage is broad, the administrators of the fund are likely to be extremely protective of the fund's meager resources in order to prevent insolvency. There will be a tendency, for example, to discourage claims against the fund, and there will be virtually no effort to give the fund the widespread publicity and educational backup that is essential if the basic purpose of encouraging employment of physically impaired workers is to be achieved.

Some states provide that if adequate funds are not available, benefits simply will not be paid. For example, North Carolina's law states: "The additional compensation and treatment expenses herein provided for shall be paid out of the Second Injury Fund exclusively and only to the extent to which the assets of such fund shall permit. . . . Should the fund be insufficient to pay both compensation and treatment expenses, then the said expenses may, in the discretion of the Commission, be paid first and compensation thereafter according to the reasonable availability of funds in the fund" (Section 97–40.1).

Evaluation of Second-Injury Funds   Despite strong evidence that disabled workers in general are dependable employees, there persists an unfavorable attitude among many employers toward hiring the handicapped, partly because of fear of increased costs resulting from such hiring. Findings of numerous surveys of employer experiences and attitudes, however, indicate that failure of handicapped workers to obtain employment is not solely a result of employers' fears of increased workers' compensation costs, a fear that second-injury funds might allay.[5] Other studies emphasize the lack of employer recognition of the purpose or even the existence of second-injury funds (U.S. Department of Labor 1961). Notable in one study was the comment of the researchers that second-injury funds may serve more as a symbol for encouraging hiring handicapped workers than as a means of providing substantial financial assistance to the hiring (Industrial Relations Counselors 1958).

Williams studied the attitudes of Minnesota employers toward hiring handicapped workers and reported that employment oppor-

---

5. Some of the studies are reviewed in greater detail in Larson (1973).

tunities may vary with the type of handicap: workers with certain impairments, such as epilepsy and back problems, will probably have a difficult time securing employment. Williams also reported that many employers question the economic value of hiring the handicapped. "Concern about increased workmen's compensation cost remains a special problem," he concluded. "At least one-third of the employers thought workmen's compensation costs would increase if they hired an epileptic; over half thought that hiring persons with back ailments would have this effect" (Williams 1971, 145).

Even though second-injury funds thus are not a panacea, some of the groups most knowledgable in this area, such as the President's Committee on Employment of the Handicapped, have strongly supported the use of the funds in encouraging the hiring of the handicapped. Recent contacts suggest that this support still exists and that the funds provide an effective tool for use with employers for promoting this worthwhile social goal.

One reason for support of the second-injury fund approach, whatever its limitations, is that the alternative ways to solve the employment problems of handicapped workers have serious deficiencies. One early attempt at a solution involved the waiver by handicapped employees of their rights under the compensation statutes. Although this procedure protects employers from increased risks, it has been considered generally unacceptable because it violates a basic principle of workers' compensation: that a worker injured on the job is entitled to medical care and cash benefits as a matter of right. The number of states with such waiver provisions has steadily declined.

Another attempted solution was that of apportionment of the liability: that is, limiting the employer's liability where a previously impaired worker is further injured to what would be paid to a fully fit worker who sustained the same injury. For example, under this approach, a worker with only one arm who loses his or her other arm in an industrial accident would be compensated only for the loss of the second arm but not for permanent total disability. While both of these approaches—waivers and apportionment—limit the liability of the employer and thus reduce the hesitancy to hire handicapped workers, both throw the burden of subsequent injuries upon the handicapped worker and his or her dependents, or on society.

A partial solution is found in the insurance mechanism itself, which, through its rate-making procedure, distributes the liability for all work-related injuries among a large number of employers who are subject to manual classification rates. However, larger employers, who employ a high proportion of workers, receive little or no assistance from this mechanism, since their rates largely or solely depend on their own experience. Self-insured employers carry their own risk (except for a portion that may be spread by excess loss insurance). Thus the protection offered by the insurance rate-making procedure seems of limited value in reducing employers' concerns about higher costs associated with hiring handicapped workers.

Still another alternative is that offered by state and federal antidiscrimination statutes. An increasing number of states have adopted provisions, within either the workers' compensation law or the general labor law, prohibiting discrimination against workers who are injured, or who file claims for compensation benefits, or who apply for employment or reemployment after becoming handicapped. In addition, the Federal Rehabilitation Act of 1973 prohibits discrimination and requires affirmative action by the federal government or its contractors in cases involving handicapped workers, and also prohibits discrimination on the basis of handicap by any recipient of federal financial assistance. Probably the most effective program providing assistance to disabled workers is the veterans' preference program, supplemented by a veterans' reemployment rights statute.

This brief review of alternative approaches to encouraging the employment of handicapped workers indicates that most have serious deficiencies, which reinforces the potential contributions of second-injury funds. Unfortunately, the limitations of second-injury fund provisions in many states have substantially reduced how effectively these funds have encouraged the employment of injured workers. For one thing, many funds have much too narrow coverage, applying only to cases where the previous impairment was the loss of a member (arm, leg, hand, foot) or of an eye. Furthermore, even when there is broad coverage of the first injury, the fund often is not operative unless the prior and subsequent injuries result in permanent total disability. Such cases are a very small proportion of all cases involving handicapped persons, since few work injuries cause the loss of a member, and less than 1 percent of all injuries result in permanent total disability. Another serious deficiency in many laws is their failure to limit the employer's liability for medical care benefits and in death cases.

Moreover, many of the funds are woefully underfinanced—often depending upon the payment of small amounts in no-dependency death cases—and the nature and purpose of the funds are not made known to the employers and employees by a widespread, continuing publicity campaign. Obviously, the inadequately financed funds are likely to be used very sparingly, as the administrators of such funds are apt to become overly protective in order to prevent their funds from becoming insolvent.

Even in those states having the most advanced type of subsequent-injury fund laws, it would be misleading to conclude that this approach provides the complete answer to the problem of employment of the handicapped. It is evident that fear of increased workers' compensation costs is only one of several reasons—and probably not the most important one—for the reluctance of some employers to hire disabled persons. Nevertheless, the role of these special funds, though limited, is an essential component of a comprehensive plan to employ handicapped workers. Where they are not used, or where the coverage is too narrow or the financing is inadequate, either the injured worker does not get the full compensation due, or the employer has to bear such high costs that employment of the handicapped is discouraged. On the other hand, where a special fund provides broad coverage for cases involving second injuries, not only is the employee more likely to be fully compensated but the fund removes an important barrier to the employment of the handicapped.[6]

Recommendations   Second-injury funds are found in all jurisdictions and should be continued. However, many do not make the maximum possible contribution to hiring the handicapped because of their limitations, and thus revisions are needed.

Second-injury funds should provide for broad coverage of preexisting impairments regardless of cause or nature. Coverage should not be limited to injuries involving the loss of a member, nor just to

---

6. The primary objective of second-injury funds is to encourage employment of handicapped workers. A secondary objective is to shift a part of the economic burden resulting from employment of handicapped workers from the hiring employer to all employers, or (in a few cases) to the state as a whole. The burden of a second disability can thus be shared more equitably. The second-injury fund does this by relieving the employer of all or part of the disability or death caused by or contributed to by a prior condition. From this perspective the fund may serve a useful purpose of spreading the risk even if it does not significantly reduce the element of discrimination against handicapped workers.

those cases where the combined result of the prior and subsequent injuries is permanent total disability. On the contrary, the fund should extend to claims arising from heart disease, epilepsy, diabetes, arthritis, or any other preexisting condition, whether the result of injury or disease, and whether occupational or nonoccupational, including congenital. It should also cover any permanent consequence, whether death, permanent total disability, or permanent partial disability resulting from the combined injuries that is substantially greater than the result of the subsequent injury itself. In order to keep the fund from being swamped with claims, a threshold level of severity for the previous impairment should be established. This minimal level will have to be determined on a state-by-state basis in order to match the permanent impairment rating standards used in the jurisdiction. The goal should be to set the threshold low enough so that workers with impairments serious enough to hinder their employment opportunities qualify for the second-injury fund, but not so low that employers can use the fund for employees who would have been hired even if the fund did not exist.

In addition to providing broad coverage, the fund should be fully publicized in order to be completely effective. Arguably, the allocation of liability between the fund and the employer should be left to the discretion of the compensation agency, so that in each case the employer pays an amount equal to the benefits due to the second injury standing alone. However, because determining the contributions of the prior and subsequent injuries to the resulting disability (especially where there is a broad coverage fund) is difficult, it is probably more desirable to make an arbitrary allocation of the employer's liability, such as one or two years of benefits, in order to avoid disputes and inordinate litigation. The additional certainty from this approach should also make risk-averse employers more willing to hire the handicapped.

The second-injury fund should have a broad financing structure, based on an assessment on all employers or insurers. A percentage either of compensation payments or of premiums charged is used in many states and has been found generally satisfactory. The use of compensation payments as a basis for assessments has the advantage of equalizing the assessments between self-insurers and employers who purchase insurance. (If the assessments are based on premiums, and self-insurers are expected to pay an assessment equivalent to what they would pay if they were insured by a carrier, this assessment will be based on an estimate of what their premiums would be, which may not be accurate.)

The compensation agency should have authority to determine the necessary level of assessments based on actuarial studies and to make adjustments in the rate without approval by the legislature. The insurance commissioner should be consulted before any assessment is made, since premium rates would be affected by the decision, and this is a matter within the jurisdiction of the insurance department. The insurance commissioner also should have the authority to audit and examine the administration of the fund.

Some funds are financed by a small assessment on employers in no-dependency death cases. These assessments do not normally provide a sufficient amount of money to carry on the fund's program but may be employed to supplement other sources. If the employer is to be assessed in such cases, the amount should not be a trivial figure, such as $100 or $500, but should reflect the average cost of a death case for a worker with dependents.

Benefit Adjustment Funds

One of the most serious deficiencies of the workers' compensation system has been its failure to keep its benefits in long-term cases in line with rising wage or price levels. Typically, compensation is awarded on the basis of the workers' earnings and the schedule of benefits in effect at the date of the injury. As a result, over the course of years the benefits fail to keep pace with the impact of inflation or of increased productivity, and the weekly benefits become seriously inadequate. One argument made to justify this situation is that the premiums collected to pay for the benefits are calculated using the payroll that existed at the time the injury occurred or when the disease was contracted, and therefore no money is available to pay for increased benefits later. The other side of the coin—that the worker, had he or she not been injured, would have continued to work and enjoy the fruits of his or her labor, with periodic wage increases to reflect increasing productivity, rising price levels, and possible promotional opportunities—is often given less weight. The disastrous consequences of frozen benefits became more acute in the 1970s as the rate of inflation accelerated.

To help remedy this serious deficiency, some states have created special funds or other arrangements to attempt to keep compensation awards more or less up-to-date. The groups most adversely affected by the failure to keep compensation benefits current are the permanently and totally disabled, survivors of deceased workers, and workers suffering from long-term and severe impairments which, while not qualifying the workers for permanent total disability benefits, nevertheless cause serious economic handicaps that may be beyond the range of rehabilitation efforts and are likely to become worse with time. Most benefit adjustment efforts have been directed toward the first two groups. The needs of the third group may be just as acute, but the much larger size of the group makes the adjustment costs higher than for the first two.

Benefit adjustments may be either retroactive or prospective, automatic or nonautomatic, and may be applicable only to permanent and total disability cases, total disability cases and death, or such cases plus permanent partial disability cases. Essentially, a retroactive adjustment provision is one that deals with cases already receiving benefits as of the date of enactment of the provision. A prospective adjustment provision deals with cases involving injuries that occur after the enactment of the provision. The financing methods vary also. Retroactive adjustments generally are paid from general revenues or a special fund; prospective adjustments may be paid either from monies pooled into a special fund, or by the individual employer or the carrier insuring the risk. Automatic benefit adjustments are those that are made on a regular, periodic basis as the result of a legislative enactment and without the need for further amendments. Nonautomatic adjustments, on the other hand, require new legislation for each adjustment. Another distinction is that sometimes the adjustment is based on changes in the wage level and sometimes on changes in the price level.

Since the cost of providing adjustments in all long-term cases across the board may be very high, especially in times of high inflation, an effort may be made either to limit the increased benefits to specific types of cases (such as permanent total disability or death) or to place a cap on the amount of the increase. (For example, even if the average wage level went up by 11 percent during the year, the benefit adjustment might be limited to a maximum or cap of 6 percent.)

Retroactive Adjustment Provisions   Retroactive adjustments with automatic updating of one or more classes of beneficiaries have been provided by 11 states, the District of Columbia, and two federal acts (see table 7.4). All of these provide for updating of permanent total disability benefits, and seven update death benefits. The benefits are paid from a special fund or an equivalent arrangement such as a segregated account in a state fund, or from general revenues. None charges the benefits to individual employers; this is because of the constitutional constraints on imposing liability retroactively on individual employers, and because these future costs could not have been foreseen when the initial employer-insurer contracts were made. In two of the states (Oregon and Washington), employee as well as employer contributions are used to help finance the benefit adjustments.

The costs of retroactive benefit adjustments that include periodic future adjustments are difficult to predict, perhaps even more so than prospective adjustments. In addition to the problems of forecasting inflationary effects on wage or price levels and on investment returns, and of the duration of payments remaining to be made after the initial adjustment, there is the additional factor of the wide range of initial differences between preadjustment and postadjustment levels of weekly benefits (some cases go back thirty or more years).

Prospective Adjustment Provisions   Automatic increases on a prospective basis, for one or more classes of beneficiaries, have been made by sixteen states, the District of Columbia, and the two federal acts (see table 7.5). Since prospective adjustments can be made by increasing the premium rate to reflect the anticipated higher costs, it is not necessary to set up separate funds. The ordinary insurance policy contract arrangement between the insurer and employer can accommodate prospective benefit adjustments, even though the exact ultimate cost cannot be predicted with complete certainty. To the extent that the prospective adjustment procedures do not involve the use of the special fund approach, they are outside the purview of this study; however, our experience to date is too limited to establish with finality that tying the cost of adjustments to the premium rate structure is a viable alternative. It is worth noting that a few states rely upon a fund to spread the cost of such adjustment either in whole or in part upon all employers. It is also worth noting that Section 55 of the Model Act published by the Council of State Governments proposes that payments for both prospective and retroactive benefit adjustments be made from a special fund.

Ad Hoc Adjustments of Benefits   In addition to the states mentioned in tables 7.4 and 7.5, seven states (California, Delaware, Maryland, Nevada, New York, Utah, and Wisconsin) have provided for limited updating of benefits on an ad hoc basis (i.e., nonautomatic and nonperiodic). For instance, California updates certain temporary total benefits whenever the maximum rate is increased by the legislature; Delaware brought old permanent total benefits up to the September 1970 level and death benefits up to the 1971 level; Maryland provided supplemental benefits for permanent total cases originating between July 1, 1965 and July 1, 1973; Nevada and Utah periodically increase benefit levels by special legislation; New York has raised old permanent total and death benefits to the July 1, 1974 level; and Wisconsin brought old total disability benefits up to the 1970 level. In each case, except for California, the supplemental benefits are payable out of a special fund. The constitutionality of the Delaware law was challenged on the ground that the claimant's right to compensation rests on the date of injury and cannot be reduced or enlarged after that. The state supreme court upheld the act in *Price* v. *All American Engineering Company* (320 A.2d 336), ruling that the provision did not violate either the contract clause or due process clause, or cause deprivation of vested property rights.

History of Benefit Adjustment Provisions   One of the earliest examples of retroactive benefit adjustment provisions was that of Oregon, which set up a retroactive benefit reserve to adjust benefits in long-term cases while the state still had its exclusive state fund. Employees and employers were charged a penny a day (eventually raised to six cents a day) to finance this reserve. Washington also had a supplemental pension fund, financed in part by contributions from both employers and employees.

In 1955 Michigan amended its law relative to benefits for certain presumptive permanent total disabilities (e.g., loss of both arms, legs, hands, feet, or eyes). Not only were such disabilities to be paid benefits for life or full period of disability, but the benefits were to be adjusted to keep pace with changes in benefits for new injuries, with the increases to be paid out of the state's second-injury fund.

In 1966, Donald L. Ream pointed out that only five states and the Federal Employees Compensation Act (FECA) adjusted benefits even in limited areas to make provision for the impact of inflation (Ream 1966). Since then, progress has been made, but slowly. Just when it seemed in the early 1970s that updating of "obsolete rates," as they are referred to in New York, was about to become an important part of workers' compensation reform in this country, the old fear of rapidly escalating costs resulting from uncontrolled inflation raised its head once more, and the persons hardest and most innocently hit by inflation—the disabled workers and their surviving dependents— were left to rely upon their own meager resources so that the program costs could be kept within acceptable limits. Now that inflation has been brought at least temporarily under control, opponents of adjustment can argue that there is no pressing need for cost-of-living increases.

Financing   The financial sources of the funds that provide for regular periodic benefit adjustments are shown in tables 7.4 and 7.5. All benefits under the FECA, and part of the benefits under the Federal Longshoremen's Act, are financed out of general revenues. Several states, including Connecticut, Delaware, Michigan, and Wisconsin, rely for financing retroactive benefits on their second-injury or multi-purpose funds.

Oregon's and Washington's financing provisions for benefit adjustments are unusual. In Oregon, every employer retains eight cents for each day or part of a day the worker is employed (Section 656.506). This money is paid to the director of the workers' compensation department and is used to finance the retroactive reserve as well as the second-injury fund. Three-fourths of the money goes to the retroactive reserve. Washington also provides for employee contributions. North Dakota periodically transfers funds from earnings on the reserve of its exclusive state fund to the supplemental benefit fund.

Evaluation of Benefit Adjustment Funds   The adjustment of benefits because of inflation for permanently and totally disabled persons and for dependent survivors of workers who die as a result of job-related injuries or diseases has been widely endorsed. The National Commission on State Workmen's Compensation Laws (1972, 64, 71, 114), reports issued by the Nixon and Ford administrations,[7] and the International Association of Industrial Accident Boards and Commissions (1983, 22) all affirmed support for the principle of upgrading benefits to protect against the impact of inflationary pressures. The case for adjustments in benefits is more persuasive because of the high rate of inflation in recent years. Over the period from 1970 to 1980, the consumer price index increased by 124 percent. This meant that a workers' compensation claimant who received a $60.00 per week award in 1970 for permanent total disability could, by 1980, buy only $26.79 worth of goods or services valued in terms of 1970 dollars. Even in the halcyon days of the early 1980s, prices were up over 20 percent in the first three years of the decade.[8]

Despite the strong support for inflation protection in benefits, as of 1980, only nineteen jurisdictions in addition to two federal acts adjusted benefits for claimants already on the rolls. In seven of those states, further adjustments would be made only if new legislation were passed in subsequent years. Seventeen jurisdictions plus the two federal acts provide protection for new cases.

The main arguments against benefit adjustments are their added costs and the difficulty of predicting the costs. More than twice the reserves are needed to provide for escalated death and permanent total disability benefits, as opposed to constant benefits if the current actuarial assumptions are used. For other types of benefits, where the average payment duration is shorter, the additional reserve requirements would be smaller.

Employers in certain high-hazard industries, such as steel erection, have high manual premium rates, sometimes exceeding $20.00 per $100.00 of payroll. These same high-hazard classes tend to have a higher proportion of serious injury cases than do low-hazard industry classes (e.g., those with less than $2.00 per $100.00 of payroll). Therefore, high-hazard industry classes will pay a higher than average percentage increment for benefit escalation.

In addition to the higher estimated costs on average needed to pay for benefit adjustments, the actual costs are subject to enormous fluctuation over time. Therefore, there can be no assurance that fu-

---

7. U.S. Departments of Labor; Commerce; Health, Education and Welfare; Housing and Urban Development, *White Paper on Workers' Compensation* (1974), pp. 4–5; and Interdepartmental Workers' Compensation Task Force (1977, 15).

8. Calculated from data in *Monthly Labor Review* (June 1984), table 19, p. 81.

ture adjustments in rates, up or down, will not be necessary, requiring future generations of employers to pay for part of the obligation incurred by an earlier generation—or possibly for future employers to receive a rebate from the excessive premiums paid by the earlier generation.

Despite the high cost and uncertainties of automatic benefit adjustments, many employers and insurers advocate automatic adjustment of certain benefits as a matter of equity and because they recognize that workers' compensation must respond to the need for protection of the value of benefits if the program is to remain viable. But they also advocate coordination with benefits from Social Security and other social insurance programs in order to preclude excessive escalation for persons who receive benefits from more than one program in the workers' disability income system.

Adjustments in benefits could be linked either to a price index or a wage index. Among the nineteen jurisdictions with prospective benefit adjustment provisions, only Ohio and Virginia use a price index (the national consumer price index). Connecticut uses the state's average production wage. All other states use state average weekly wages from the state employment security programs as the basis for adjustments. An advantage of the wage index is that one is available for each state. In contrast, the consumer price index is available only for the nation and for certain metropolitan areas.

If the purpose of automatic benefit adjustments is to maintain purchasing power, this concept is more accurately measured by a price index than by a wage index. On the other hand, if the purpose of the workers' compensation benefits is to replace a portion of the worker's lost earnings, it is more appropriate to make benefit adjustments based on a wage index. Some employee representatives have advocated adjustments based on a wage index, as such an index represents more accurately the wage changes the disabled worker would have received had he or she remained active in the labor force. Insurance representatives have advocated adjustments proportional to price index changes, arguing that the only purpose was to protect against losses of purchasing power.[9] Most of the recommendations cited ear-

---

9. These suggestions were made in response to option papers prepared by the staff of the Interdepartmental Workers' Compensation Task Force in 1976. Quite likely the responses would be different at a time when price level changes outstrip wage level changes for many workers.

lier in this section would base the benefit adjustments on changes in wages rather than prices.

Ten of the jurisdictions that have adopted prospective automatic adjustments have incorporated the projected cost into the insurance premiums collected during the year when the injury occurred, thus creating reserves to pay for future benefit escalation. Nine other states use special funds to pay for the cost of benefit adjustments on a current basis.

An argument in favor of the special funds approach is that the rate of inflation is beyond the control of individual employers, and therefore benefit adjustments because of inflation should be financed by taxing the general public or by assessing all employers at a flat rate based only on payroll without regard to hazard classification differentials. The special funds approach also has the attribute of lower initial costs, although obviously in the long run the assessments to pay the benefit adjustments will have to increase.

Alternative methods of softening the immediate cost impact of benefit adjustment legislation have been proposed. One alternative would build into the premiums enough reserves to cover projected future benefit changes for only five years into the future. Under this alternative, premium rates would be adjusted each year to provide sufficient money to adjust benefits one more year into the future.

Another suggestion would create a special fund to pay only for that part of future benefit adjustments that exceeds a predetermined level. Thus the fund could pay for the part of any adjustment that exceeds 5 percent in one year; the rest of the adjustment, if necessary, would be built into the rate structure.

Representatives of some self-insuring employers have advocated use of general tax revenues to finance future benefit adjustments. Insurance representatives feel that most, if not all, of the cost should be built into the rate structure in order to create sufficient reserves in advance to pay for adjustments. However, they support a maximum annual adjustment factor or, alternatively, public funding of any excess adjustment over a stipulated percentage in a given year.[10]

Another issue regarding benefit adjustment concerns whether or not only certain types should be adjusted, such as permanent total disability benefits and death benefits.

---

10. See fn. 9.

Any claimant who receives benefits for more than one year in an inflationary economy would benefit from automatic adjustment. There are three types of benefits that are likely to continue for more than fifty-two weeks: death, permanent total disability, and major permanent partial disability. Most beneficiaries receive benefits for less than one year for other types of workers' compensation benefits, although a very small percentage of temporary total cases continue beyond a year of disability.

Many employee, employer, and insurance representatives are in substantial agreement that death and permanent total disability benefits should be automatically adjusted. Employee representatives advocate coverage for long-term permanent partial beneficiaries as well, while insurance and employer representatives generally advocate exclusion of permanent partial beneficiaries unless they are substantially out of the labor market.[11]

Whether adjustments should be made periodically, or whether they should be triggered by a predetermined change in the index to which they are tied is also an issue. Changes that are made annually, on a predetermined date, are more readily subjected to actuarial calculations and can be administered more efficiently. A more conservative recommendation is to defer the initial adjustment until the first adjustment date that occurs twenty-four or more months after the injury. Having a waiting period of two years before beneficiaries are eligible for adjusted payments would reduce costs by eliminating short-term claims from the adjustment program.

Finally, the question is asked whether workers' compensation beneficiaries who also receive Social Security disability benefits should receive automatic benefit adjustments. Social Security disability benefits are reduced by the amount that combined workers' compensation benefits and disability benefits exceed 80 percent of the claimant's base weekly wage. The base weekly wage is adjusted triennially to reflect changes in the cost of living, and the offset is adjusted so that combined benefits will not exceed 80 percent of the adjusted base wage. Should the workers' compensation benefit be increased by a greater percentage than the base wage, the Social Security benefit would be reduced. If the reverse is true, the Social Security benefit would be increased up to the 80 percent limit.

---

11. See fn. 9.

It can be argued that, where beneficiaries receive both kinds of benefits, Social Security, rather than workers' compensation, should absorb the expense of cost of living expenses, since the federal government is more responsible for inflation and able to cope with it than are states, employers, or carriers. If, in the presence of dual benefits, Social Security would accept responsibility for all inflation adjustments, workers' compensation costs would be reduced. However, this approach would compromise the principle of internalized workers' compensation costs.

Insurance representatives have advocated careful coordination of Social Security and workers' compensation benefit adjustments to assure that additional beneficiaries do not receive multiple adjustments, as is now possible in most states for persons who receive death benefits from both Social Security and workers' compensation.

Recommendations   Periodic adjustment of benefits to keep them in line with the cost of living is essential to a modern workers' compensation program. The laws should provide benefits that take actual loss of earning power of the injured worker into account, and thus a wage index should be used as a basis for adjustments.

Benefit increases cannot readily be financed retroactively—for a worker already on the rolls at the time of the law's amendment—by direct charges against his or her employer. This is because the premiums for coverage of such a worker have already been paid. A special fund should be used for financing these costs, based on an assessment on all employers or insurers, that would not impose an excessive burden on any one employer.

Prospective benefit adjustments for new cases could be financed by being included in premiums, by use of a special fund, or by a combination of these approaches. Prospective adjustments should be made automatically, on an annual basis, in proportion to increases in the state's average weekly wage. We recommend that the amount necessary to provide such adjustments be included in the premium rates, and that the state insurance authorities carefully review the trend and projection factors employed in setting the rates so as to ensure that the increases in premiums are proportionate to the amount of escalated benefits actually paid out. Carriers should not be pemitted to build in excessive safety margins, based on overly conservative assumptions such as high rates of inflation and low rates of return on reserves, that create unjustified cost burdens for employers and discourage adoption of such provisions.

Special Funds for Occupational Diseases

The previous discussion indicates that special funds play a useful role in buttressing the normal financial mechanism in workers' compensation. Second-injury funds, the most prevalent type of special funds, improve the prospects of employing the handicapped while also spreading the costs of such employment among all employers. Benefit adjustment funds, which recently have become more common, help protect workers against inflation while limiting the uncertainty to employers and carriers of providing the protection.

The contributions of these relatively well-established funds provide a background for our conclusion, which considers work-related diseases as a problem than can benefit from an expanded use of special funds. Only seven states had funds specifically devoted to the problem in 1980.

The lack of special funds for occupational diseases is not surprising because until recently diseases were considered a minor factor in workers' compensation. Just a decade ago the National Commission on State Workmen's Compensation Laws devoted only two pages to the topic in its report (1972, 50–51). It is unimaginable that a similar report issued in the 1980s could deal with occupational diseases in such a facile fashion because of three interrelated developments that have occurred in the last decade: first, a growing awareness that the magnitude of the work-related disease problem is substantially greater than previously recognized; second, increasing concern about how the workers' compensation program can deal with occupational diseases; and third, increasing discussion of programs other than workers' compensation that could protect workers afflicted by occupational diseases.[12]

As the consciousness of occupational diseases has been rising, one aspect that has become evident is that the long latency period associated with many diseases makes it especially difficult to identify causal relationships with employment in general and with individual employers in particular. A related aspect is that when a responsible employer or carrier is identified as the source of a slow-starting dis-

---

12. For an extended discussion of these developments, see Burton (1981).

ease, there may be insufficient financial reserves to provide benefits. These factors pose problems for employers, employees, and, more generally, the normal financial mechanism in workers' compensation.

Current Special Funds for Occupational Diseases   Several states have attempted to deal with these problems by using the special fund approach. New York amended its law in 1946 to limit the liability of employers whose workers incur certain slow-starting illnesses, such as silicosis and other dust diseases. Generally until 1974, the employer's liability was limited to the first 260 weeks of total disability. In 1974, partial disability was also recognized as compensable, and the employer's liability was limited to the first 104 weeks of benefits, with compensation payments beyond that duration reimbursed by the special disability fund.

In Colorado, if an employee becomes disabled with silicosis or asbestosis, or if the employee is poisoned, or develops a disease or malignancy, or dies because of exposure to radioactive materials, substances, machines, or fissionable materials, and if the employee had been injuriously exposed to the source of these disorders while in the employ of another employer, then the last employer or carrier is liable only for disability, death, and medical benefits up to $10,000, and any additional benefits are payable out of the subsequent-injury fund.

Kentucky also limits the liability of the last employer in certain occupational disease cases where the exposure in the last employment was for less than five years. In all silicosis or pneumoconiosis cases, and all other occupational diseases that develop to the point of disability only after an exposure of five or more years, compensation for disability or death as a result of such diseases shall be paid jointly by the employer and the special fund—the employer being liable for 60 percent of the compensation and the special fund for 40 percent of the compensation.

Michigan's Silicosis and Dust Disease Fund reimburses carriers or self-insurers for weekly benefits, after a total of $12,500 has been paid in accordance with the act, to employees disabled as a result of occupational silicosis or other dust disease on or after May 1, 1966. If two or more employers have been paying benefits to an employee whose disabled condition falls within the fund's provisions, reimbursement is to be made to the employee's last employer after combined weekly payments exceed $12,500. Reimbursement is made whether the disability is total or partial. Like the state's second-injury fund, financing is by annual assessments against total workers' disability compensation benefit payments made by insurance companies, self-insured employers, and the state accident fund during the prior year, exclusive of medical, rehabilitation, and funeral benefits. As of December 31, 1979, the fund had 858 payment files, with another 115 claims awaiting reimbursement following payment of $12,500 by the employer. During 1979 the fund was added by motion to 443 litigation cases, and an additional 62 cases were referred to the fund by the employer or insurance carrier to consider for voluntary reimbursement.

The Pennsylvania Occupational Disease Compensation Act provides that

> ...when a claimant alleges that disability or death was due to silicosis, anthraco-silicosis, coal workers pneumoconiosis, asbestosis or any other occupational disease which developed to the point of disablement only after an exposure of five or more years, the only employer liable shall be the last employer in whose employment the employee was last exposed to the hazard of such occupational disease during a period of six months or more: And provided further, that in those cases where disability or death is not conclusively proven to be the result of such last exposure, all compensation shall be paid by the Commonwealth.

Where liability or death is due to the last exposure, the employer is liable for 60 percent of the compensation due and the commonwealth for 40 percent.

Wisconsin provides that benefits becoming due after ten years from the date of injury or last payment of compensation for occupational diseases (or twelve years from the date of injury or last payment of compensation for lung diseases or diseases caused by exposure to a toxic substance or to ionized radiation) shall be paid from the work injury supplemental benefit fund.

California has provided since January 1, 1981 for the payment of benefits to asbestos workers disabled as a result of asbestosis from a special account established within the Uninsured Employers Fund. The Asbestos Workers' Account is used to pay benefits where a claim is filed for workers' compensation and the employer cannot be located or fails to pay compensation within thirty days. The worker must file an application before the Workers' Compensation Appeals Board, prior to the first payment of benefits by the Asbestos Workers' Account, to determine the responsible employer for the payment of compensation. The account is administered by the director of industrial relations and is financed by continuing appropriations, beginning with an initial appropriation of $2,625,000. The account is to take all reasonable and appropriate steps to insure that the account recovers the money paid as benefits and costs.

The California fund initially limited payments to temporary disability and medical benefits, but subsequently expanded to include permanent total disability and death benefits. Nonetheless, through the end of 1983 only thirty-seven cases had been accepted that accounted for a total cost of $274,000, and half of these were for medical benefits only (Woodward 1984). One expert on the California experience has speculated that the low utilization of the fund is largely a result of the widespread reliance on tort litigation by workers exposed to asbestos (Woodward 1984). This approach is often used because for asbestos cases, the "probability of recovery seems substantially greater under the tort liability system than under even 'purposely liberalized' workers' compensation programs" (Woodward 1984). Because of the unique aspects of asbestos-related diseases, and in particular the extensive utilization of tort suits by afflicted workers, the limited use of the special fund in California cannot be considered indicative of the potential contribution of special funds to solving the problems associated with compensating work-related diseases in general.

Evaluation and Recommendations   Evaluation of the current occupational disease funds is complicated because of the small number of funds, which typically cover only one or a few diseases. The paucity of use of the California fund appears to be related to the unique status of asbestos-related diseases. In contrast, the Michigan experience indicates that such funds can receive considerable use.

The case for increased use of occupational disease funds rests not on the proven success of such funds but on the compelling evidence of the difficulties the workers' compensation program is having with the compensation of work-related diseases. Barth (1980) has documented the delays, extensive litigation, and considerable reliance on compromise and release agreements associated with occupational disease claims. While there are multiple causes of these aberrations, the long latency period of certain diseases is an important determinant. Strengthening the case for the special funds is the inappropriateness of some of the traditional methods used to deal with long latency, such as statutes of limitations that require claims to be filed within a limited period after the date of last exposure to the toxic substance. These limiting features found in many state laws have been documented by Larson (1979).

We recommend the use of a special fund to assume some or all of the liability for occupational disease claims filed a significant period after the year of last exposure to the causative factor. (This exposure date normally determines which carrier or employer is responsible for the benefits.) As an example of the appropriate period, Burton (1981) proposed that a disease protection fund assume responsibility for some or all of the payments for benefits when the claim is filed five or more years after the end of the policy year that defines the responsible carrier.[13]

The provisions defining the precise nature of an occupational disease fund will have to be developed for each state on the basis of policy decisions such as the scope of the statutory definition of work-related diseases and whether some or all of the diseases covered by the statute are also encompassed by the special fund. Although the task of designing an occupational disease fund will be formidable, we believe the effort is justifiable given the inherent problems of dealing with work-related diseases within workers' compensation, the defects of other solutions to these problems, and the documentation we have provided of the general success of special funds in ameliorating some of the weaknesses in the normal financing mechanism for workers' compensation.

---

13. The Burton proposal would establish a separate fund to compensate all diseases contracted by workers regardless of the origin of the diseases, and thus does not represent a special fund in workers' compensation as we have defined that term. However, much of the discussion of the financing of the Disease Protection Fund (Burton 1981, 23–25) is relevant for the present study. For one reaction to the Burton proposal, see Joseph (1983, 318–21).

TABLE 7.1
Special Funds in Use as of 1980 by Jurisdiction

State or Jurisdiction	Second Injury	Uninsured Employers	Insolvent Carriers	Insolvent Self-Insurers	Benefit Adjustment	Extended Medical Care	Rehabilitation	Continuation of Payments	Occupational Disease	Reopened Cases	Other	Total
Alabama	x		x									2
Alaska	x		x				x					3
Arizona	x	x	x	x		x	x					6
Arkansas	x		x					x				3
California	x	x	x						x		x	5
Colorado	x		x			x	x		x			5
Connecticut	x	x	x	x	x		x					6
Delaware	x		x		x							3
Dist. of Col.	x		x		x		x				xxx	7
Florida	x	x			x		x					4
Georgia	x		x									2
Hawaii	x	x	x		x							4
Idaho	x		x									2
Illinois	x		x		x							3
Indiana	x		x					x				3
Iowa	x		x									2
Kansas	x	x	x	x							x	5
Kentucky	x	x	x						x			4
Louisiana	x		x									2
Maine	x		x									2
Maryland	x	x	x									3
Massachusetts	x		x									2
Michigan	x		x	x	x				x		x	6
Minnesota	x	x	x	x	x	x		x	x			8
Mississippi	x		x									2
Missouri	x		x				x					3
Montana	x	x	x				x					4

State												Total
Nebraska	x		x				x					3
Nevada	xᵃ	x	n.a.				x					3
New Hampshire	x		x	x								3
New Jersey	x		x	x								2
New Mexico	x		x									2
New York	x	x	x	x	x	x	x				x	10
North Carolina	x		n.a.									2
North Dakota	xᵃ	x	n.a.		x		x				x	4
Ohio	xᵃ	x	n.a.	x								4
Oklahoma	x		x									2
Oregon	x	x	x	x			x					6
Pennsylvania	x	x	x					x			x	6
Puerto Rico	x	x	n.a.	n.a.								3
Rhode Island	x		x		x		x					3
South Carolina	x		x								x	3
South Dakota	x		x									2
Tennessee	x		x									2
Texas	x		n.a.	n.a.								2
Utah	x		x	x		x	x					5
Vermont	x		x									2
Virginia	x	x	x	x								3
Washington	xᵃ	x	n.a.	x	x		x				x	6
West Virginia	xᵃ	x	n.a.	x	x		x				x	4
Wisconsin	xᵃ		x	x					x		x	6
Wyoming	x	x	n.a.	n.a.							x	3
U.S.												
FECA	xᵃ	n.a.	n.a.	n.a.	n.a.							1
LHWCA	x	x	x		x		x				xxx	7
Black Lung											x	1
Total	54	21	44	11	18	4	17	4	7	2	19	201

Source: Responses to inquires to state workers' compensation agencies supplemented by analysis of state laws and reports.

Note: n.a.: not applicable.

a. Arrangements for second injuries provided by exclusive state insurance funds or (under FECA) government self-insurance.

TABLE 7.2
Methods of Financing Second-Injury Funds
(1980 data)

State	Method of Financing
Alabama	$100 in death cases; $25 fine for late reporting; interest on bonds.
Alaska	8% of compensation payments for permanent partial disability; $10,000 in no-dependency death cases.
Arizona	Not to exceed 2% of premiums and self-insurer costs; $1,250 in no-dependency death cases.
Arkansas	$500 in no-dependency death cases.
California	Appropriation; death benefit payments.
Colorado	No-dependency death cases.
Connecticut	Assessments of 3.5% of compensation paid against employers and carriers (may be more than one assessment a year).
Delaware	Premium assessments (not to exceed 1%) plus self-insurer assessments.
Dist. of Columbia	Prorated assessments on carriers and self-insurers based on total compensation and medical payments; $5,000 in no-dependency cases; fines and penalties collected under the act.
Florida	Assessment on insurer premiums and equivalent costs of self-insurers; investments.
Georgia	Assessment on carriers and self-insurers; in no-dependency death cases, half the sum payable to a dependent or $10,000, whichever is less; penalties assessed under act.
Hawaii	Assessment on carriers and self-insurers.
Idaho	Not to exceed 4% of certain benefits awarded or paid.
Illinois	$500 in loss of member cases and $1,000 in death cases.
Indiana	1% assessment on total compensation paid.
Iowa	$1,000 in death cases (triggered on when fund drops below $50,000 and off when fund reaches $100,000).
Kansas	General revenues; assessment on insurers and self-insurers; $5,000 in no-dependency death cases.
Kentucky	0.75% assessment on the amount of premiums or "adjusted cost"; additional assessments may be levied if necessary.
Louisiana	1% on premiums written by carriers; equivalent assessment on self-insurers.
Maine	100 times state's average weekly wage, in no-dependency death cases.
Maryland	5% assessment on all awards for permanent disability or death, and settlement cases.
Massachusetts	$500 in death cases; $500 additional in no-dependency death cases; assessments on insurers and self-insurance.
Michigan	Assessments based on 175% of total disbursements from fund, less net assets in fund exceeding $200,000.
Minnesota	$5,000 in death cases where there are no dependents or less than $5,000 due in benefits; 7% of compensation payments, adjusted according to balance in fund.
Mississippi	$500 in no-dependency death cases; $150 in other death cases.

TABLE 7.2 (continued)

State	Method of Financing
Missouri	Assessments on all benefits paid.
Montana	Assessment of up to 5% of prior year's compensation; $1,000 in death cases.
Nebraska	1% assessment on insurer premiums or self-insurer equivalent.
Nevada	Assessment on premiums and self-insurers.
New Hampshire	Assessment on insurers and self-insurers.
New Jersey	Assessment on insurers and self-insurers.
New Mexico	$1,000 in no-dependency death cases and assessment not to exceed 1% of compensation benefits other than medical and attorneys' fees.
New York	Assessment on carriers and self-insurers.
North Carolina	$25 payment in cases involving loss of minor member, and $100 in cases involving 50% or more loss of major members.
North Dakota	From premiums (state fund).
Ohio	From premiums (state fund).
Oklahoma	2% assessment on total compensation paid for permanent total and permanent partial disability, plus 2% deducted from awards to employees for permanent disability; assessments suspended when fund reaches specified amount.
Oregon	Premiums and employer assessments; employee assessment; interest.
Pennsylvania	Assessments based on total compensation paid.
Puerto Rico	From reserve fund for disasters maintained by state insurance fund.
Rhode Island	2.75% assessment on gross premiums received by carriers, or equivalent amount on self-insurers; $750 in no-dependency death cases.
South Carolina	Prorated assessments on all carriers and self-insurers, based on total compensation paid.
South Dakota	0.50% assessment on all compensation payments; $500 in no-dependency death cases; payments suspended when fund reaches specified amount.
Tennessee	$150 in each death case and $15 in each permanent partial disability case.
Texas	Full death benefits in no-dependency death cases, but not to exceed 360 weeks of compensation.
Utah	$15,600 payment in no-dependency death cases.
Vermont	$500 in no-dependency cases.
Virginia	0.25% assessment on premiums.
Washington	From state accident fund monies; assessment on self-insurers.
West Virginia	From employer premiums into state fund and investments.
Wisconsin	Payments in scheduled injury and death cases.
Wyoming	Assessment in no-dependency death cases; appropriations from state's general fund.

Source: State statutory provisions; information received from state compensation agencies.

TABLE 7.3
Second-Injury Funds:
Operating Statistics of Selected States as of 1980

State	Fiscal Year	Employer or Insurer Payments	Other Payments into Fund	Payments from Fund	Current Balance of Fund	Claims Accepted	Claims Rejected	Claimants Receiving Benefits
Alabama	1979	$ 130,575	$ 68,920 (interest)	$13,527	$1,025,161	2	0	5
California	1979–80	2,258,935	none	3,969,138	350,862	476	n.a.	1,945
Delaware[a]	1980	1,240,594	0	1,253,390	13,648	102	n.a.	153
Florida	1979	11,262,880	n.a.	18,738,647	12,616,836	n.a.	n.a.	n.a.
	1980	n.a.	n.a.	n.a.	11,393,748			
Hawaii[b]	1980	3,649,396	183,380	1,047,056	3,254,572	317	n.a.	600
Idaho	1980	286,861	83,649 (primarily interest)	119,011	1,217,722	16	Fund must defend each claim	19
Illinois	1980	331,968	6,913 (interest)	409,135	33,412	8	n.a.	142
Indiana	1979		none	339,677	204,273	11	none	83
Iowa	1980	26,100	9,957 (interest on investments)	61,273	58,087	6	n.a.	6
Kansas[c]	1980	2,653,436	1,695,796	2,390,215	2,578,528	n.r.	n.r.	n.a.
Louisiana	1979	2,033,000	none	834,222	1,400,000	64	40	c. 80
Massachusetts	1980	457,358	none	742,642	339,184	n.a.	n.a.	n.a.
Michigan[d]	1979	14,152,000	none	8,953,000	4,334,399	n.a.	n.a.	1,581
Montana	1979	none	2,000	15,277	1,916,072 (includes short-term investments)	1	0	0
Nebraska	1980	none	53,507	53,672	477,677	2	6	16
Nevada[e]	1980			444,331		91		
New Hampshire	1978	none	2,519	46,281	1,693	57	n.a.	36 (15 insurers)

State	Year							
New Jersey	1979	12,568,836	none	9,995,573	5,327,089	839	701	2,999
New York	1979	26,271,699	1,933,912	21,132,363	18,881,004	n.r.	n.r.	n.r.
North Carolina	1979–80	27,425	n.a.	31,441	104,375	3	n.a.	6
North Dakota[f]	1980	n.a.	n.a.	6,414	225,000	n.r.	n.r.	c. 10
Ohio[f]	1978			7,381,846 (charged to surplus)		3,699		
Oregon	1980	4,367,651	881,784 (interest)	4,709,317	7,596,151	526	9	c. 526
Pennsylvania	1979	40,600	0	48,782	199,434	18	n.a.	18
South Carolina	1979–80	2,031,262	372,044	1,556,532	1,192,817	497	n.a.	1,288
South Dakota	1979	54,005	0	18,404	75,531	0	0	3
Vermont	1980	500	0	6,706	17,814	0	0	1
Washington[f]	1980	2,813,096	14,927 (pension reserves (deposit interest) transferred to fund)		207,070	32	n.a.	n.a.
Wisconsin[g]	1978	1,188,609		232,993	1,842,472			

Source: Information received from state compensation agencies and annual reports.

Notes: n.a.: not applicable.

n.r.: not recorded.

a. Includes payments for benefit adjustments in certain cases, as well as for second injuries.

b. Hawaii: special compensation fund provides payments for several purposes including second injuries. Payments from fund shown are second injuries.

c. Kansas: 430 claims against the fund, with 138 awarded benefits.

d. Michigan: includes payments for handicapped workers, additional benefits to statutory permanent and total disability cases, and in certain appealed cases. Payments do not include administrative costs.

e. Nevada: has an exclusive state fund, which does not charge the cost of claims involving subsequent injuries to the employer for experience-rating purposes. Subsequent-injury fund set up within state fund, with assessments against self-insurers.

f. exclusive state insurance fund.

g. Work injury supplemental benefit fund provides payments for several purposes, payments from fund shown are for second injuries; other figures are for entire fund.

TABLE 7.4
Retroactive Benefit Adjustment Provisions
in U.S. Jurisdictions (effective in 1980)

Jurisdiction	Types of Benefits Adjusted		Financing Source	
	Permanent Total	Death	Special Fund	General Revenue
Connecticut	x		x	
District of Columbia	x	x	x[a]	x[a]
Florida	x		x	
Illinois	x		x	
Michigan	x		x	
Minnesota	x		x	
New Hampshire	x		x	
North Dakota	x	x	x	
Ohio	x		x	
Oregon	x	x	x[b]	
Washington	x	x	x[b]	
West Virginia	x	x	x	
FECA	x	x		x
LHWCA	x	x	x[a]	x[a]

Notes: These jurisdictions retroactively adjust certain benefits for regular periodic adjustments to keep benefits in line with current rates.

a. One-half of benefit adjustment for injuries occurring prior to November 26, 1972, are payable out of a special fund and one-half from appropriations.

b. Includes contribution from workers.

TABLE 7.5
Prospective Benefit Adjustment Provisions
in U.S. Jurisdictions (effective in 1980)

Jurisdiction	Types of Benefits Adjusted			Basis for Adjustment		Financing Source	
	Permanent Total	Death	Permanent Partial	Wage Index	Price Index	In Premium	Special Fund
Connecticut	x[a]	x		x		x	
District of Columbia	x	x		x		x	
Florida	x						x
Hawaii	x						x
Idaho	x		x[b]	x		x	
Illinois	x	x		x			x
Maine	x	x	x[b]	x		x	
Michigan	x			x			x
Minnesota	x[a]	x		x		x	
New Hampshire	x[a]			x		x[c]	
North Dakota	x	x		x			x
Ohio	x	x	x		x		x
Oregon	x[a]	x		x			x[d]
Vermont	x		x[b]	x		x	
Virginia	x[a]	x			x	x	
Washington	x[a]	x		x			x[d]
West Virginia	x	x	x	x		x	
FECA	x	x					x[e]
LHWCA	x	x		x		x	

Notes: a. Also temporary disability.

b. Also temporary partial disability.

c. For injuries occurring on or after July 1, 1975.

d. Includes contribution from workers.

e. From general revenues.

8 · CHALLENGES TO WORKERS' COMPENSATION: AN HISTORICAL ANALYSIS

Edward D. Berkowitz and Monroe Berkowitz

In the recent literature on workers' compensation, the emphasis has been on sophisticated econometric analysis. This analysis allows us to measure the performance of workers' compensation and to discover ways in which the program relates to other disability programs. It also permits a glimpse into such important questions as whether workers' compensation insurance premiums have a strong influence over safety in the workplace.[1] Within the literature, however, there is also a place for analysis that describes the program in more qualitative terms. Although this sort of analysis has also become a staple of workers' compensation literature over the years, it often tends to be descriptive rather than prescriptive: it offers no visions of the future. Much of it also has a static quality; it seldom explains the origins of the phenomena under discussion.

This chapter makes an attempt at institutional analysis of a different sort. We seek to define and to explain the program's institutional strengths and weaknesses by exposing the program to historical analysis. In particular, we wish to examine the challenges that have threatened the program's existence and the responses the program has made to those challenges. In this manner we hope to use the past as a means of reflecting upon the future. Is the program

---

1. See, for example, Chelius (1977) and Worrall (1983).

likely to remain in place? In what ways is it likely to be altered in the future?

We organize our effort around three sets of challenges. The first concerns the disparity between the aspirations of the program's founders and the realities of the program's performance. The second involves the program's position within the larger American social welfare system. As a state program, it faces criticism from social planners who feel that occupational disability is a challenge that can only be addressed on the national level. Workers' compensation, according to this view, clutters the institutional landscape and inhibits efforts at reform.

The third challenge comes from shifting society's expectations for the goals of disability programs. When workers' compensation began, income maintenance was considered its primary objective, and the structure of workers' compensation reflected a desire to achieve that objective. As medical technology improved, however, it became possible to contemplate rehabilitating instead of merely compensating the victims of industrial accidents. This new possibility posed a stiff challenge to workers' compensation.

After analyzing the challenges to workers' compensation, we then examine recent events, placing particular emphasis on the reforms advocated by the National Commission on State Workmen's Compensation Laws. From an examination of the way that the states responded to the commission's recommendations, we detect important future trends, trends that make us sanguine about the future survival of workers' compensation, even in the face of the challenges we present.

Challenge One: Aspirations and Reality

What is puzzling about workers' compensation laws is that they ever appeared at all, let alone that all of the states adopted them between 1911 and 1948. At one time, historians thought they had a convincing explanation for the mass acceptance of these laws between 1911 and 1920. During this so-called progressive era, an outpouring of societal concern over the excesses of industrial activity occurred, and reformers succeeded in passing laws that provided protection for the worker against the risk of industrial accidents. (Bremner 1956; Weiss 1918–35, 3:565ff.). Newer research suggests a disparity between the rhetoric of the reformers and the reality of the situation. As a result of this disparity, the laws failed to live up to the expectations that the reformers created for them and that attracted a great deal of criticism initially.

Workers' compensation acted as a no-fault insurance law that required the employer to buy insurance to cover the risks of industrial accidents that occurred in his plant. The program replaced a more informal system in which workers attempted to recover damages by initiating a lawsuit. According to available evidence, workers were beginning to enjoy considerable legal success at the beginning of the compensation era. In contrast to the early nineteenth-century experience, juries were showing a marked sympathy toward maimed employees, much as current juries do not hesitate to find medical doctors guilty of malpractice (Posner 1972).

Why, then, did reformers make such an effort to remove the system from the courts? One answer is that reformers attributed a great deal of uncertainty to the court system, an uncertainty that added to a more general feeling that the entire industrial system was out of control. As might be expected from a system that depended on the findings of a jury considering only the case before it, awards varied greatly from case to case. One worker might receive an amount adequate to cover his or her losses; another worker, with exactly the same disability, might receive nothing. Reformers continually exposed new evidence that highlighted the capricious results of the court system. The Pittsburgh Survey, an influential examination of industrial conditions, revealed that the families of workers who died in industrial accidents received no compensation in 88 of 304 cases that arose between 1907 and 1908 (Eastman 1910). A commission investigating the situation in New York found that workers received payments from the courts in only one of every eight accidents. The reformers desired a system in which every accident received consideration.[2]

Delays in settling cases also received considerable attention from reformers who regarded these delays as a serious shortcoming of the court system. Delays caused social problems, as injured workers sought income and medical care to tide them over until they received their settlements.

---

2. Remarks of Mr. Boyd in *Compensation for Industrial Accidents: Conference of Commissions* (1910, 22).

The literature of reform, therefore, highlighted instances of delay and made it appear to be an inevitable element of the court system. In a report prepared by an Illinois commission (Employers' Liability Commission for the State of Illinois 1910, 12–13) investigating the problem of industrial accidents, vignettes appeared that emphasized the delays in particular cases. One such anecdote told of a worker who fell into a vat of hot water in the city of Chicago on July 29, 1905. Although he eventually recovered $2,000, he had to endure one trial and two appeals, and never received his money until December 22, 1909. Here was a case, then, in which the system left the worker without assurance of a settlement for nearly four years. Another worker caught his arm in a belt on October 11, 1903. Six years and one month later, he received $11,083.

Still another element of the court system that disturbed reformers centered on the coercive power of insurance companies. The insurers gave workers the hope of circumventing the court system and receiving prompt settlement. For that reason, of 279 fatal accidents that occurred in the railroad industry in Illinois around 1910, 185 of them reached settlement out of court. Reformers feared that these settlements, almost always of the lump sum variety, failed to compensate the workers adequately (Employers' Liability Commission 1910, 12–13). In the contest between workers and insurance companies, workers often found themselves at a disadvantage (Gersuny 1981, 69–70).

Reformers also argued that judges and juries failed to give work accident cases the careful consideration they deserved. As a result, they reached incorrect decisions and failed to consider the actual needs of the workman in making awards. More human weaknesses entered the system as well, such as being less generous to immigrants than to native Americans (Gersuny 1981, 69–70).

The reformers may have suffered from a time lag. Distracted by the cases of injustice, discrimination, and delay, reformers may not have realized the courts were becoming more sympathetic and that jury awards were increasingly favorable to the injured workers. Perhaps it is inevitable that the reforms of today are based on the perceived abuses of yesterday, whatever the merits of the perception.

The reformers' critique of the court system determined the nature of workers' compensation. Under the new system, all injured workers were to receive compensation without the litigation and other sources of delay and antagonism found in the tort system. Although benefit amounts might be less than those awarded by the courts, benefits came to all injured workers as a matter of right. Still, there existed a need for a modern, specialized agency to replace the courts, and the reformers invented such an agency. They called it the Industrial Accident Board or Industrial Commission. According to the proponents of workers' compensation, "The members of the board become specialists. They get to understand problems that arise under the administration of the law . . . they work out a uniform administration of the law" (U.S. Congress 1914, 43).

The word *specialist* was central to the progressive critique of the óld court system. The members of the new Industrial Commission would be specialists in a way that the judges simply were not. Specialists were experts in solving problems and free from the financial pressures of the insurance companies and the prejudices that animated judges and juries (see Wiebe 1962, 4).

Expectations surrounding the new laws and the new agencies created to administer them were, therefore, very high. The new system was supposed to eliminate litigation since the level of benefits was now specified by law, and it was also intended to eliminate much of the antagonism between worker and employer that threatened to disrupt the very fabric of American society. The problem of industrial disability had been solved through the legislative process.

History does terrible things to the ideals and aspirations of reformers. The new program could not possibly have fulfilled everyone's expectations. The device of the industrial commission, like any political device, responded to the interests of the people who selected the commission members. To use the modern language of regulatory politics, commissions could be "captured" by interests antagonistic to the reformers' goals or filled with people who lacked expertise in solving the problems of industrial accidents. Dodd (1936), in his painstaking study of workers' compensation done in the mid-thirties, illustrated how politics had corrupted the system in Illinois and New York. Officials who heard disputed cases owed their appointments to politicians. The board did not automatically become a board of specialists.

The content of the laws, as well as their administration, posed potential problems that soon were realized. Workers' compensation allowed workers to receive 66⅔ percent of their average weekly wages as a benefit rate during periods of disability. It did not take long for the benefits to become outmoded, since in almost all cases the states included maximum levels for benefits. As time passed, these maximums prevented workers from receiving the 66⅔ percent of their average wages that the law promised them.

In addition, the substitution of workers' compensation laws for the court system drew criticism away from the courts and toward workers' compensation. The rhetoric of reformers to the contrary, the new system provided plenty of opportunities for disagreements that often led to hearings being held on a particular case. Contested cases raised many of the same problems for the new system that litigation had posed for the old. Administrative hearings created a delay while both sides assembled the necessary witnesses to appear on their behalf. The problems of industrial disability were too subtle for a single set of rules; cases arose in which people disagreed over the relevance or the application of a particular rule. Furthermore, the question of the degree to which a person was disabled yielded no easy answers. It was a matter of opinion whether a particular person was partially or totally disabled, or whether, for example, he or she had lost the use of a finger. Disagreement meant the possibility of a contested case; a contested case slowed the compensation process. Finally, the insurance companies, whether benevolent or malevolent, remained important to the workers' compensation system. Although the rules of industrial disability may have changed, the agent who compensated the workers stayed the same.

In sum, not all the dissatisfactions over society's approach to industrial disability disappeared upon passage of the new laws. Instead, the target of dissatisfaction shifted from the courts to the workers' compensation program; since the reformers had sold the reform in such absolute terms, the performance of workers' compensation seemed all the more disappointing.

Challenge Two: Other Social Welfare Programs

Although limitations in workers' compensation laws became apparent almost immediately, the laws survived. The reason for this survival was the lack of a politically feasible alternative. Whatever the faults in workers' compensation, few people suggested a return to the court system. The workers' compensation system was criticized for failing to transcend some of the problems of the court system, not because the new program performed worse than the old one. Other alternatives to workers' compensation involved the creation of new, more ambitious social welfare programs to cope with industrial disability. In theory, the possibility existed of creating a federal law for this purpose: substituting governmental financing mechanisms for the partnership between private employers and private insurance companies, and even absorbing workers' compensation into a more inclusive federal program of health and disability insurance. In time, each of these possibilities was to receive serious consideration and to pose a new round of challenges to workers' compensation. In the years following the progressive era, however, these alternatives failed to exist in a practical sense. They violated too many preconceptions about the proper role of government in American life.

In order to gain a sense of the government's limitations in the 1920s and 1930s, we must remember that the focus of concern in the progressive era was the workplace. Workers' compensation laws were a response to what the progressive reformers envisioned as a battle between management and labor in which the reformers acted as mediators between the two sides. The laws did not undermine the power of the private sector; instead, they sought to condition some of the ways in which business was done in order to create a more humane and, ultimately, more productive workplace. The notion that the government could go beyond the role of mediation or do more than establish minimum standards, that it could itself supply social welfare services, took many years to arise. In the meantime, workers' compensation remained at the cutting edge of social welfare programs.

Even at the start of the New Deal, workers' compensation remained a valued model. The appointment of Frances Perkins as Franklin Roosevelt's secretary of labor illustrated the importance of workers' compensation. Her claim to the job came from her experience with labor laws, and workers' compensation in particular, rather than from long experience with labor unions or the politics of labor relations. Perkins had served as a member of the Industrial Board in New York and as that state's industrial commissioner. As secretary of labor, she showed great interest in monitoring state workers' compensation laws and persuading states to make their benefits more liberal (Martin 1976, 173–79).

The importance of the workers' compensation program was

also revealed by its influence over proposed new labor laws (Martin 1976, 224). Workers' compensation served as an important precedent for Social Security and unemployment compensation. Arthur Altmeyer, the Department of Labor official most responsible for the Social Security Act in 1935, served first as secretary of the Wisconsin Industrial Commission. He was primarily a workers' compensation administrator (Nelson 1969).

Even though Frances Perkins and Arthur Altmeyer looked with sympathy on workers' compensation, the passage of the Social Security Act created new possibilities for social welfare laws. The act contained federal incentives for the creation of state unemployment compensation laws and the beginnings of a federal old-age insurance program. The challenge to workers' compensation in these new laws was not immediate. In many ways, the federally spawned unemployment compensation programs resembled workers' compensation programs. The old-age insurance program, though different in concept than workers' compensation, remained limited in its operations. Like workers' compensation, it covered mainly industrial workers and other wage or salary-earning employees; like workers' compensation as well, it relied upon a division of responsibility between workers and employers. The government collected money for old-age insurance from payroll taxes, not from a more general form of taxation. The new law, like the old one, made no charge upon general revenues. Instead, it relied entirely on the premiums collected from workers and employers.

In a more practical sense, the challenge posed by old-age insurance was muted by the gradual way in which the program was scheduled to begin. Although the legislation was passed in 1935, workers and employers were not to begin paying taxes for two years, and the monthly benefits were not slated to reach the first eligible retired workers until 1942. The Social Security Act expanded the range of the nation's social welfare laws, but it left an important role for workers' compensation in the social welfare system.

As the Social Security Board began to create an adminstrative apparatus for the new law, the need arose to find qualified personnel. One source of personnel included people with expertise in workers' compensation (Altmeyer 1932 and 1968). There was, in other words, a continuity of personnel and ideas between the workers' compensation laws of the progressive era and the Social Security laws of the New Deal.

Events after 1935 broke this connection, and the division of responsibility between workers' compensation and Social Security widened. A new generation of analysts began to study the problems posed by health and disability. Uninhibited by the restrictions imposed on government during the progressive era, they proposed different types of programs. Perhaps the most influential of the new analysts was I. S. Falk, an expert in the field of public health. His job performing research for the Social Security Board gave him an important influence over the government's future plans. In his studies, Falk (1936) began to question the purpose of dividing occupational and nonoccupational disability. Whether a disability occurred on or off the job, it created the same difficulties; Falk wondered if perhaps the same program should deal with both types of disabilities. Falk also disliked the way that workers' compensation handled the provision of health care. Industrial doctors were faced with a conflict of interest in declaring someone disabled and in determining when he or she should return to work.

Falk and his fellow planners on the Social Security Board used their studies as the basis for proposals to create two new types of disability laws. One was a temporary disability law, covering workers' incapacities that lasted from eight days to twenty-six weeks, and the other law covered chronic or permanent disabilities. Unsure of exactly where to fit the proposed new laws into the mechanisms that administered the established old ones, Falk decided to unite temporary disability with unemployment insurance at the state level and to merge permanent disability with old-age insurance at the federal level. The new proposals still provided room for workers' compensation, but the field was becoming more crowded (Falk 1936, 307–19, and 1937).

The Social Security Board proposals of the late 1930s reflected an ambivalence over whether the state or the federal government should administer social welfare laws. By the end of the decade, however, this ambivalence tended to be resolved in favor of federal laws. This resolution, in turn, posed the first serious challenge for the state workers' compensation laws.

The contents of the 1939 amendments to the Social Security Act underscored the emerging differences between Social Security and workers' compensation. The amendments broadened the benefits available under Social Security. For the first time, workers would be able to receive survivors' and dependents' benefits from the federal government. Even more important, the amendments made Social Security less of an actuarial and more of a social welfare operation. Social adequacy considerations predominated as the relationship between the amount of money a worker paid into the system (his or her premium) and the amount of money he or she received from the system (his or her benefit) became more obscure. Two workers with the same record of earnings and labor force participation no longer received the same level of annual benefits. Instead, married workers received more than single workers. In the event of a worker's death, the family of a worker who left behind a dependent received more than the family of a single worker (Berkowitz 1983b). None of these features severed the relationship between Social Security and workers' compensation, but they weakened the insurance elements that Social Security had inherited from workers' compensation.

At the same time, proponents of Social Security expansion began to suggest that eventually the system might reach the point where general revenues would be required to finance it. If that were to be the case, the Social Security system possessed the potential of becoming a major source of income redistribution from the young to the old or the rich to the poor. It would then be a very different program from workers' compensation, which still used the market elements of insurance to protect workers injured in the course of employment.

These emerging differences mattered only to the extent that Social Security entered into the field of disability and, even then, on whether the Social Security Board decided to preempt workers' compensation laws. In the discussions that preceded the passage of the 1939 amendments to the Social Security Act, Altmeyer claimed he had no interest in abandoning workers' compensation. Instead, he called the relationship between workers' compensation and Social Security "a basic question of social policy. We feel it is best to place the burden of industrial accidents where it belongs—under workmen's compensation." ("Minutes of Advisory Council Meeting" 1938). These same discussions revealed that the passage of a federal disability law lay in the future. On balance, the Social Security Board shied away from the problems of disability. One actuary, for example, said that there "were so many variables in the discussion that he could not possibly give one estimate and maintain his personal integrity." "It seems almost inevitable," he said, "that when men are laid off and cannot work, with nothing in sight, no earning power whatever, they will be judged disabled."[3] Not completely comfortable with the prospect of running a national, permanent disability law, the Social Security Board, now renamed the Social Security Administration, waited until well into the 1940s before making a serious attempt to pass the law.

Even when the serious effort to pass the law began, it still took time to bring permanent disability insurance to congressional passage. In the intervening years, workers' compensation remained the nation's major social insurance law dealing with disability. It had, however, long since lost its special position as a model for other laws to follow. The Social Security Administration no longer regarded the question of the relationship between its disability law and workers' compensation as a serious one. The administration did not attempt to preserve a niche for workers' compensation; it only attempted to guard against the duplication of benefits. All in all, it appeared that federal laws of the type envisioned by the Social Security Administration represented the wave of the future; in time, they might replace the older and less useful workers' compensation laws.

Permanent disability insurance under Social Security became law in 1956, after an exhausting and ultimately unsuccessful campaign to get the measure through the Senate Finance Committee and a dramatic fight on the floor of the Senate (Berkowitz 1979). By this time the threats to workers' compensation came not only from Social Security but from new private health and welfare plans as well. In the 1940s, employers' contributions to Social Security increased at nearly twice the rate of employers' contributions to workers' compensation (Pollack 1953, 53).

Together the private health plans and the public social security program issued a forceful challenge to workers' compensation. The new system eliminated (or so it was hoped) the last vestiges of the old court system. No longer would the question of whether a disability was work related be allowed to slow the process of compensation. Since the federal government provided an underpinning for the private-public system, benefit levels would tend to remain uniform from place to place. Just as workers' compensation replaced the court system, therefore, the new public-private system would replace workers'

---

3. W. R. Williamson, quoted in Berkowitz (1983b, 146).

compensation. Workers' compensation survived this second major challenge posed by the passage of Social Security Disability Insurance for different reasons than those that enabled it to surmount the first challenge. Confronted with the program's shortcomings in the initial years of operation, proponents could claim that workers' compensation represented the best available alternative. The new challenge could not be met in the same way. In a more cynical way, proponents could only emphasize that, bad as workers' compensation might be, it was already in place. The new programs represented untested approaches to the problem of disability. In a real sense, the survival of workers' compensation amounted to a victory only for bureaucratic inertia. Eveline Burns captured the reality behind the endurance of workers' compensation when she commented, "This was labor's first great victory . . . and they just love it and wouldn't give it up" (Burns n.d.).

The substitution of workers' compensation for the courts did not undermine anyone's bureaucratic domain. The courts were flexible, multipurpose agencies whose role in American life was assured. Workers' compensation agencies, by way of contrast, were rigid and specialized. They resented losing influence and fought to preserve their domain. Yet even in the face of this defensive behavior, workers' compensation still lost influence. Once Social Security legislation was passed, the laws played a less important role in the American social welfare system than they had previously.

Challenge Three: Rehabilitation and Changing Expectations

The rise of the federal disability program underscored the fact that people's expectations of the government had changed by the 1950s. No longer was the government's role restricted to aiding people who became the victims of unforeseen emergencies, such as industrial accidents. Now the government, the federal government in particular, took as its responsibility the provision of a foundation of security for an individual throughout his or her life. In this atmosphere of changed expectations, people looked to the government to serve more functions than it had during the progressive era. In the disability field, the increased reliance on the government coincided with a major change in the technology of caring for disability. Disability programs were no longer expected to fill only the negative function of compensating an injury; they now had the obligation to gain the benefits of modern technology and to repair or rehabilitate the injured person.

In a perverse way, war greatly benefited the development of rehabilitation. Just as passage of the original Vocational Rehabilitation Act was spurred by World War I, the experience of World War II demonstrated rehabilitation's potential. Working under intense pressure, doctors developed a new specialty, one that helped many battle casualties to return to active service and nearly normal lives after the war. The rehabilitation doctors such as Henry Kessler and Howard Rusk shared a common set of ideas; they believed an injury should be dealt with quickly and that a patient be treated not just with regard to his or her particular medical diagnosis but also with regard to minimizing the residual effects of the injury. In language popularized by Rusk, rehabilitation treated the "whole man": it served as the third phase of medicine, following prevention and treatment.

The nation embraced the ideals of rehabilitation eagerly. They appeared to illustrate the best aspects of the American character: mastering technology for peaceful and constructive purposes. Even better, it appeared to work, and it gained the sort of accolades usually reserved for major breakthroughs such as the invention of the polio vaccine. Dramatic demonstrations of rehabilitation's potential abounded after the war. Harold Russell, wounded during the war, won an Oscar for his performance in *The Best Years of Our Lives*. The award testified to people's appreciation for the degree to which he had been rehabilitated as much as for his natural, but less than professional, acting ability (E. Berkowitz 1981, 24–25).

The popular enthusiasm over rehabilitation created the expectation that workers injured on the home front should also receive rehabilitation. It fell to workers' compensation, as the comprehensive program for industrial injuries, to integrate the concept of rehabilitation into its opeations. Created to prevent injuries by imposing costs on employers and to compensate injuries once they occurred, workers' compensation needed to step outside of its historical identity in order to take on the new task.

A consensus developed among workers' compensation officials that to save the program, workers' compensation should take on the function of rehabilitation. In the Somerses' analysis of the program in the mid-fifties, they emphasized the necessity of uniting rehabilitation and compensation. Although the idea generated enthusiasm, it proved difficult to implement (Kessler 1949, 168; American College of Surgeons 1952; "Rehabilitation Committee Report" 1955, 24–25; Somers and Somers 1954).

The difficulties persist to the present day. An official at one of the major automobile companies claims he is batting zero in placing supposedly rehabilitated workers in jobs (in Berkowitz 1984). This same official worries over the profusion of rehabilitation facilities in eastern Michigan. He fears they offer expensive care that still fails to limit the compensation costs his company must pay. Recently the state of Ohio decided to offer rehabilitation facilities as part of its state insurance fund. The rhetoric of an article describing the new rehabilitation program in Ohio gives a sense of how uncertain an operation rehabilitation can be. "Anyone having a valid, compensable workers' compensation claim, who has not recovered sufficiently to return to work," the article notes, can participate in the program. Still, not everyone makes a good rehabilitation candidate. One needs a physical and mental state that suggests "a reasonable probability of rehabilitation." Not all injured workers present this probability. Participation is voluntary, and while there is no penalty for not participating, only workers with "a firm commitment" can participate. Although a good idea, rehabilitation appears exceptionally difficult to put into practice (Dell 1983). Insurance carriers, workers, and employers all have difficulty converting the potential of rehabilitation into performance. Workers' compensation, after all, was not designed to provide rehabilitation.

When rehabilitation first became popular, observers such as the Somerses thought it held the potential to revitalize the workers' compensation program. This revitalization has failed to happen. By the early 1960s, the reality of the situation became apparent to many observers of the program. Perhaps Earl Cheit (1961, 4) put it best when he said that, "the enthusiasm which launched workmen's compensation in 1910 had in large part turned to cynicism by the 1960s." By the 1960s, therefore, workers' compensation faced the brunt of the challenge from the federal disability programs and from the rehabilitation movement as well. The decade marked the program's nadir. Its survival continued to hinge upon its refusal to liquidate itself and on the failure of federal planners to move an ambitious set of federal disability and rehabilitation programs through Congress.

Responding to the Challenges: Contrasting Efforts at Reform

In the 1960s, all three of the challenges we have discussed affected workers' compensation. The program had failed to live up to the expectations created for it by its founders; it had been superceded by a system of federal Social Security and private health insurance that improved on its performance, at least in theory, by not differentiating between occupational and other types of disability; it had difficulty incorporating the latest technological advances made by rehabilitation medicine. These challenges led to a de facto loss of the program's importance. As early as the 1950s, efforts to reform workers' compensation met with indifference and even hostility. Yet, in the space of twenty years, the situation changed, and workers' compensation once again began to be viewed as a program worthy of reform. With the survival of the program assured, the various interests began to reinvest their energies in improving it. The result was a partial response to the three challenges that had arisen over the years.

The efforts of Undersecretary of Labor Arthur Larson illustrated the futility of reform efforts during the Eisenhower years (see Berkowitz and Berkowitz 1984). Since workers' compensation was not a model program, Larson believed that the states required a model law as an inspiration to improve their programs.

Instead of sparking a round of reform in the states, the model law aroused fears that the federal government was seeking to control the state programs by mandating minimum standards. On May 29, 1956, for example, the *Journal of Commerce* commented that "the Larson proposal is a type of welfare measure and one which would be financed by a very narrow segment of taxpayers." Workers' compensation, in other words, could not achieve the same broad welfare purposes of Social Security since in the *Journal's* view, only employers and not employees paid for the older law. Both Richard Nixon and Wilton B. Persons, an assistant to President Eisenhower, expressed their concern over the matter. Even a federal official in a responsible position with a passionate concern for the improvement of workers' compensation could no longer act as an effective force for reform. Much had changed since the era of Frances Perkins.[4]

The politics of social welfare overwhelmed Arthur Larson and the Eisenhower administration. The next Republican administration, by way of contrast, achieved considerable success in serving as an inspiration for the improvement of workers' compensation. In the intervening years, the politics of social welfare had changed considerably. During the 1960s a new generation demonstrated its concern for the environment. Intellectually, the 1960s and the progressive era at the beginning of the century shared common themes. During both eras, reformers perceived society as an organic whole; the actions of the poor affected the environment in which the rich lived. All groups shared this environment, and no one group had the right to ruin it for everyone else. Pollution, for example, was initially viewed as a private act but quickly became seen as a public one. Voters gave the state the right to restrict this private act in the interest of society as a whole. In both the progressive era and the 1960s, therefore, reformers saw individual acts as contributing to society as a whole, and in both eras reformers, acting in the name of the public interest, took steps to discipline individual actions.

In the sixties, a coalition of Naderites, upper-class environmentalists (whose respectable roots could be traced back at least as far as Theodore Roosevelt), trade unions, and others petitioned Congress to solve the vaguely defined problems of occupational health and safety. Acting with characteristic caution, Congress took until the end of the decade to pass the Occupational Safety and Health Act (OSHA 1970).[5] The act gave the federal government the power to regulate standards for safety and health in the workplace. State regulations remained in place only if they conformed to OSHA standards. The new law stopped short of recommending reform of workers' compensation, which also played a role in the health and safety of the workplace. It did, however, concentrate attention on the law's performance, and in typical style, rather than facing the reform issue,

---

4. Michael J. Quill to Dwight D. Eisenhower, December 14, 1953; Arthur Larson to James Mitchell, August 9, 1954; Clara Beyer to Mr. Gilhooley, January 25, 1954; all in RG 174, Records of the Department of Labor, Mitchell, Files of Arthur Larson, National Archives.

5. PL 91–596.

it suggested the creation of the National Commission on State Workmen's Compensation Laws.

As political commentator Elizabeth Drew (1968) has noted, national commissions often serve as convenient ways to sweep a problem under the rug. They function as lightning rods that draw attention away from the president and the Congress. The commissions that work best, according to the conventional wisdom of the academy, are those that provide an opportunity for opposing parties to meet and to fashion a political compromise. Something of this sort happened with the National Commission of State Workmen's Compensation Law (Berkowitz 1983a).

Chaired by an academician, John F. Burton, Jr., the commission itself consisted of eighteen members with representatives from the insurance industry, the workers' compensation administrators, the medical and legal professions, and the labor unions, as well as public and political members. Ceremonial appointments of people with no experience in workers' compensation were kept to a minimum. The commission brought together the various interests involved in workers' compensation. Unlike Larson's interdepartmental committee, it provided a true forum for a reform proposal to come from the interests themselves, rather than from a group of external federal experts. The commission was not vulnerable to charges that its recommendations failed to comprehend the difficulties of interest-group politics. With a professional staff of twenty and a panoply of experts, consultants, and contractors, the commission undertook "a comprehensive study and evaluation of state workmen's compensation laws in order to determine if such laws provided adequate, prompt, and equitable system of compensation." A final report containing "a detailed statement of the findings and conclusions of the Commission together with such recommendations as it deemed advisable" was to be transmitted by the commission to the president and Congress no later than July 31, 1972.

Not only did the commission succeed in meeting its deadline, it also produced a unanimous report. The interests found that they were able to agree on a set of suggestions for the reform of the state laws. The only disagreements concerned matters of emphasis. The labor representatives wanted the Congress to pass federal workers' compensation legislation immediately; others preferred to wait and see how the states would respond to the commission's recommendations. Both sides agreed on issuing a set of standards for the states to follow.

The commission took the further politic step of designating certain of its recommendations as essential. It gave the states three years to adopt the recommendations. After that time, it recommended that compliance be evaluated: if the states were found not to have instituted the standards, Congress was requested to take steps to guarantee compliance without further delay. Here then was a true compromise: labor agreed not to demand immediate federal legislation, in return for management's assurance that if the states failed to act in three years, then management would join labor in calling for federal legislation.

In the meantime, both sides agreed that the essential recommendations should include the following: compulsory coverage with no occupational or numerical exemptions, full coverage of work-related diseases, full medical care and rehabilitation services without limitations as to time or dollar amount, and specific objective standards on benefits. In addition, the commission included recommendations that went back to the origins of workers' compensation. Temporary total benefits were recommended to be no less than two-thirds of a worker's average wage, subject to a maximum weekly benefit of at least two-thirds of the state's average weekly wage by July 1, 1975. The commission made similar recommendations on death benefits and permanent total benefits (National Commission 1972).

The states failed to meet the commission's recommendations, but Congress failed to pass legislation. In this sense, the commission's report did not lead to a fundamental turning point in the history of workers' compensation. Compared to the response generated by Larson's model workers' compensation law, however, the commission report represented a major force for change in the state laws. Only six of fifty-two jurisdictions had temporary total maximum weekly benefits that were two-thirds of the state's average weekly wage in 1972. By 1983, thirty-two of the fifty-two met the standard and even higher proportions met the recommended standards in the permanent total and death cases. The Department of Labor periodically issued measures of state compliance with the nineteen essential recommendations of the commission. The average score of the fifty-two jurisdictions went from 6.9 in 1972 to 12.2 in 1983, and the proportion of the work force covered by workers' compensation rose four percentage points in the same period (U.S. Department of Labor, ESA-OWCP, n.d.; U.S. Department of Labor 1981).

The commission's essential recommendations failed to deal with the more complex aspects of the three challenges to workers' compensation. In a sense, they marked a response to the first challenge; they brought the program's aspirations for benefit levels closer to its actual performance. As for the challenges posed by other disability programs and by rehabilitation, the commission's essential recommendations stopped short of responding to them. Complicated matters like rehabilitation, occupational illnesses, and permanent partial disabilities could not be solved in a manner that could be monitored by the Department of Labor. As a consequence, these complex matters were set aside; moreover, they did not adapt themselves well to the process of political bargaining that characterizes national commissions.

For all of the limitations of the commission's work, it provided a striking contrast to Larson's earlier efforts. Perhaps the difference lay in the contrast between the two eras. In the 1970s, it became clear that federal programs had as much difficulty coping with the complexities of disability as did workers' compensation. Permanent partial disabilities were still not formally covered by the Social Security Program; temporary disabilities of any sort proved difficult for the federal program to handle. During the early eighties, for example, a furor erupted when the Reagan administration attempted to reexamine disability insurance recipients to determine if they were still disabled. The decision to grant disability benefits under federal law, it became clear, amounted in many cases to an award of lifetime benefits. Furthermore, federal income maintenance programs enjoyed no great success in rehabilitating their beneficiaries. By the seventies, therefore, one could no longer contrast the known defects of workers' compensation with the promises of federal programs. The contrast between aspiration and reality that had once posed a challenge to workers' compensation now affected the federal program as well. The result was a lessening of all three of the challenges to workers' compensation.

With the challenges to the existence of workers' compensation no longer so pressing, and assisted by the efforts of the National Commission to initiate the reform process, the states began to grapple with the more fundamental problems on their own. Signs began to point to a reversal of the trend toward diminished influence of workers' compensation among social welfare programs. The trend persists. The total cost for employers of workers' compensation, running at 1 percent of payroll or a little over during the 1960s and early 1970s, now hovers close to 2 percent of payroll. Benefits paid are increasing at the rate of 30 percent or more every two years. The approximately $3 billion paid in benefits in 1970 increased to $13.4 billion in 1980. Although all social insurance benefits increased during this period, workers' compensation increased faster. For example, total disability expenditures in the United States reached 25.3 billion in 1970 and increased 150 percent to 63.5 billion in 1977. Workers' compensation, by way of contrast, increased almost 200 percent during the same period.

In this atmosphere where actions in the workers' compensation field appear to have consequences, state after state has reformed its laws. In New Jersey, the interest groups managed to agree on a more restrictive definition of disability in exchange for the liberalization of the forty-dollar-a-week maximum benefit for permanent partial disability that had existed in that state's law for a long time. Florida substituted a wage loss system for a previous system of payment for permanent partial disabilities that had long been recognized as containing glaring deficiencies. Nevada accomplished long sought changes separating the judicial from administrative functions. Michigan passed laws dealing with the problems of compromise and release settlements, and the awarding of benefits to workers who retired. The list of accomplishments could be extended to other problems and other states.[6]

This list of accomplishments does not imply that all problems have been solved or that the future of workers' compensation is assured. Although we have not stressed the problem of occupational disease, this issue continues to plague the workers' compensation system. As one company official notes (Berkowitz 1984), workers' compensation does a good job with the "blood trail" injuries. Occupational illnesses and diseases are far more subtle. They have a slow onset,

---

6. For the increases in the workers' compensation payments, see Burton and Berkowitz (1980), "The Role of Workers' Compensation Programs in Promoting Occupational Safety and Health," in chapter 1, table 1.2. The data are taken from Daniel Price's periodic articles in the *Social Security Bulletin*. For the increases in disability insurance payments generally, see Monroe Berkowitz (1981) and Department of Labor (1983).

and they pose grave health hazards to workers who contact them. The link between employment and the illness or disease often becomes difficult to establish.

At the present time, the Miller bill occupies the attention of the compensation community.[7] This bill deals with asbestosis, and proposes to take this disease away from the state workers' compensation system and to place it under the administrative control of the federal government. Representative Miller calls asbestos disease a "national tragedy of stunning proportions." He notes that the workers' compensation system will pay only 5 percent of the medical costs involved. He claims that the inadequate nature of the compensation system has driven many workers to bypass it altogether, and to file lawsuits against manufacturers and other third parties. If the Miller bill should become law, it would represent a significant erosion of the state workers' compensation program.

Conclusions

As the example of the Miller bill makes clear, the process of challenge and response is far from over. History illustrates the dynamic tendencies of social welfare programs over time. A crisis causes society to create new laws to deal with occupational disability. In time the new law generates its own problems; it gets superceded by a newer law which in turn meets a new set of difficulties. In the case of workers' compensation, its problems have contributed to the creation of federal disability laws and to special federal laws that represent limited takeovers of workers' compensation responsibilities. The federal black lung legislation illustrates one area in which states have yielded completely to the federal government. Selective inroads on workers' compensation seem destined to continue as society continues to locate new sources of occupational disability and environmental hazards. And just as the shortcomings of federal laws have increased interest in workers' compensation, they have also focused attention on the courts, the historical layer that lies beneath workers' compensation. Society may decide that the courts should exercise greater responsibility in this area than they do at present.[8]

---

7. HR 3175, introduced by Representative Miller on May 26, 1983.
8. The Arizona law, for example, permits an action at law for damages if the injury is caused by the employer's or the employee's willful misconduct.

Above all, this account of the challenges to workers' compensation demonstrates the durability of the program, its ability to survive in the face of extraordinary challenges and, in recent years, to meet the challenges head-on. This process of accommodation should continue in the years ahead.

Reviewing the challenges to workers' compensation, we find that the state programs have been best able to meet the first one. A cycle of reform and indifference has appeared over the years, a cycle that can be endlessly repeated as economic and political climates continue to change. The second challenge, that posed by federal disability and other social welfare programs, has resulted in the creation of new responsibilities at the federal level and selective ceding of responsibility from the state workers' compensation laws. This process also appears likely to continue. The move toward federal financing and control no longer looks to be unidirectional. The Reagan experience suggests that power can flow back to the states, although the American system of public finance favors the ability of the federal government over the other branches of government to raise revenues.

The third challenge, that of rehabilitation, may be the most difficult for workers' compensation to surmount. Technology, unlike politics, does not yield easily to a cyclical pattern. A program created in one era experiences great difficulty in incorporating the state of the art technology from the next era. Workers' compensation may simply have to abandon the rehabilitation effort, and yield to a new generation of public and private rehabilitation programs. The meshing of rehabilitation with the economic and administrative constraints of public programs poses an extraordinarily complex problem. Perhaps the next round of technological change will lower the unit cost of rehabilitation, although that prediction runs counter to recent trends in the field of medical care.

For the immediate future, we are confident that the workers' compensation program will survive. This outcome is a positive one in and of itself, for it means that the time and energy once devoted to discussions of the extinction of the program can now be devoted to its improvement.

BIBLIOGRAPHY

Abramowitz, Milton, and Stegun, Irene A.
    1964   *Handbook of Mathematical Functions.* Washington, D.C.: National
            Bureau of Standards.
Advisory Council on Social Security
    1979   *Reports of the 1979 Advisory Council on Social Security.* Washing-
            ton, D.C.
Akerlof, George A., and Dickens, William T.
    1982   "The Economic Consequences of Cognitive Dissonance." *Amer-
            ican Economic Review* 72, 3(June 1982):307–19.
Altmeyer, Arthur J.
    1932   "The Industrial Commission of Wisconsin." *University of Wis-
            consin Studies in the Social Sciences and History.* Madison: Uni-
            versity of Wisconsin Press.
American College of Surgeons
    1952   *Bulletin* (July 28, 1952). Records of the Vocational Rehabili-
            tation Administration, RG 363 Accession 71A-1382, Carton
            65. Washington, D.C.: National Records Center.
Armstrong, Barbara
    1932   *Insuring the Essentials.* New York: Macmillan.
Arrow, Kenneth J.
    1981   "Risk Perception in Psychology and Economics." Technical Re-
            port no. 35 (October 1981). The Economic Series, Institute for
            Mathematical Studies in the Social Sciences. Stanford, Calif.
Bartel, Ann P., and Thomas, Lacy Glenn
    1982   "OSHA Enforcement, Industrial Compliance, and Workplace
            Injuries." Working Paper no. 953. Cambridge, Mass.: National
            Bureau of Economic Research.
    1985   "Direct and Indirect Effects of Regulation: A New Look at
            OSHA's Impact." *Journal of Law and Economics* (April 1985).

Barth, Peter S., with H. Allan Hunt
    1980   *Workers' Compensation and Work-Related Illnesses and Diseases.*
            Cambridge, Mass.: MIT Press.
Bem, D. J.
    1967   "Self-Perception: An Alternative Interpretation of Cognitive
            Dissonance Phenomena." *Psychological Review* 74, 3:183–200.
Berkowitz, Edward D.
    1979   *Disability Policies and Government Programs.* New York: Praeger.
    1981   "The Federal Government and the Emergence of Rehabilita-
            tion Medicine." *Historian* 43(August 1981):24–25.
    1983a   "Commissioning the Future, Getting the Present." *Reviews in
            American History* (June 1983):294–99.
    1983b   "The First Social Security Crisis." *Prologue* (Fall 1983):133–49.
    1984   Interview conducted by Edward D. Berkowitz with officials of
            the Ford Motor Company. Detroit, Michigan. May 21, 1984.
Berkowitz, Edward D., and Berkowitz, Monroe
    1984   "The Survival of Workers' Compensation." *Social Service Review*
            58, 2(June 1984):259–80.
Berkowitz, Monroe
    1973   "Workmen's Compensation Income Benefits: Their Adequacy
            and Equity." In *Principles of Workmen's Compensation*, vol. 1,
            *Supplemental Studies for the National Commission on State Work-
            men's Compensation Laws*, edited by Monroe Berkowitz, 189–
            274. Washington, D.C.: Government Printing Office.
    1981   "Social Policy and the Disabled." In *Social Security Issues and
            Disability Issues in Policy Research*, 1–23. Geneva: International
            Social Security Association.
Berkowitz, Monroe, and Burton, John F., Jr.
 forthcoming *Permanent Disability Benefits and the Workers' Compensation Pro-
            gram: A Multistate Study of Criteria and Procedures.* Kalamazoo,
            Mich.: W. E. Upjohn Institute for Employment Research.
Borgida, E., and Nisbett, R. E.
    1977   "The Differential Impact of Abstract vs. Concrete Information
            on Decisions." *Journal of Applied Social Psychology* 7, 3(July–
            September 1977):258-71.
Bremner, Robert H.
    1956   *From the Depths: The Discovery of Poverty in the United States.* New
            York: New York University Press.
Brown, Charles
    1980   "Equalizing Differences in the Labor Market." *Quarterly Journal
            of Economics* 94, 1(February 1980):113–34.
Burns, Eveline M.
    1956   *Social Security and Public Policy.* New York: McGraw-Hill.
    n.d.   Interview. Columbia Oral History Project.
Burton, John F., Jr.
    1981   "The Challenge of Diseases for Workers' Compensation." Pa-

per presented at the Seminar on Current Issues in Occupational Diseases. City College of New York, November 16, 1981.

Burton, John F., Jr., and Berkowitz, Monroe
1980   "The Role of Workers' Compensation Programs in Promoting Occupational Safety and Health." Unpublished report prepared for the Occupational Safety and Health Administration, October 1980.

Butler, Richard J.
1983   "Wage and Injury Rate Response to Shifting Levels of Workers' Compensation." In *Safety and the Workforce: Incentives and Disincentives in Workers' Compensation,* edited by John D. Worrall, 61–86. Ithaca, N.Y.: ILR Press.

Butler, Richard J., and Worrall, John D.
1983   "Workers Compensation: Benefit and Injury Claims Rates in the 1970s." *Review of Economics and Statistics* 65 (November 1983):580–89.
1985   "Work Injury Compensation and the Duration of Nonwork Spells." *Economic Journal* (September 1985).

Cheit, Earl F.
1961   *Injury and Recovery in the Course of Employment.* New York: Wiley and Sons.

Chelius, James R.
1974   "The Control of Industrial Accidents: Economic Theory and Empirical Evidence." *Law and Contemporary Problems* (Summer/Autumn 1974):700–729.
1977   *Workplace Safety and Health: The Role of Workers' Compensation.* Washington, D.C.: American Enterprise Institute.
1979   "Economic and Demographic Aspects of the Occupational Injury Problem." *Quarterly Review of Economics and Business* 19, 2(Summer 1979).
1982   "The Influence of Workers' Compensation on Safety Incentive." *Industrial and Labor Relations Review* 35, 2(January 1982):235–42.
1983   "Workers' Compensation and the Incentive to Prevent Injuries." In *Safety and the Workforce: Incentives and Disincentives in Workers' Compensation,* edited by John D. Worrall, 154–60. Ithaca, N.Y.: ILR Press.

Chelius, James, and Smith, Robert S.
1983   "Experience Rating and Injury Prevention." In *Safety and the Workforce: Incentives and Disincentives in Workers' Compensation,* edited by John D. Worrall, 128–37. Ithaca, N.Y.: ILR Press.

Coase, Ronald
1960   "The Problem of Social Cost." *Journal of Law and Economics* 3(October 1960):1–44.

Compensation for Industrial Accidents: Conference of Commission.
1910   Chicago, November 10, 1910. Boston: George Ellis Printers.

Conley, Robert, and Noble, John
1979   "Workers' Compensation Reform: Challenge for the 80's." In *Research Reports of the Interdepartmental Workers' Compensation Task Force*, vol. 1. Washington, D.C.: Government Printing Office.

Connolly, Terry, and Gilani, Neveed
1982   "Information Search in Judgment Tasks: A Regression Model and Some Preliminary Findings." *Organizational Behavior and Human Performance* 30(1982):330–50.

Council of State Governments
1963 and   *Workers' Compensation and Rehabilitation Law.* (Model Act). Lex-
1965   ington, Ken.

Cox, D. R.
1972   "Regression Models and Life Tables." *Journal of the Royal Statistical Society*, series B, 34(1972):187–220.

Dawson, Marshall
1940   *Problems of Workmen's Compensation.* Bulletin no. 672. Washington, D.C.: U.S. Department of Labor, Bureau of Labor Statistics.

Dell, Bob
1983   "Ohio's Commitment to Disabled Workers." *Comprehension* (Fall 1983).

Dickens, William T.
1984a   "Occupational Safety and Health Regulation and Economic Theory." In *Labor Economics: Modern Views*, edited by William Darity. New York: Kluwer-Nijhoff.
1984b   "Differences between Risk Premiums in Union and Non-union Wages and the Case for Occupational Safety Regulation." *American Economic Review* 74, 2(May 1984): 320–23.

Dillingham, Alan E.
1981   "Sex and Age Characteristics of the Labor Force and Their Relationship to Workers' Compensation Costs." Paper presented at the Seminar on Incentive and Disincentive Issues in Workers' Compensation Insurance. City College of New York, November 16, 1981.

Dodd, Walter F.
1936   *Administration of Workmen's Compensation.* New York: Commonwealth Fund.

Doherty, N.
1979   "National Insurance and Absence from Work." *Economic Journal* 89(March 1979):50–63.

Dorsey, Stuart
1983   "Employment Hazards and Fringe Benefits: Further Tests for Compensating Differentials." In *Safety and the Work Force: Incentives and Disincentives in Workers' Compensation*, edited by John D. Worrall, 87–102. Ithaca, N.Y.: ILR Press.

Dorsey, Stuart, and Walzer, Norman
    1983   "Compensating Differentials and Liability Rules." *Industrial and Labor Relations Review* (July 1983):642–54.

Downey, E.H.
    1924   *Workmen's Compensation.* New York: Macmillan.

Drew, Elizabeth B.
    1968   "On Giving Oneself a Hotfoot: Government by Commission." *Atlantic Monthly* (May 1968):47.

Eastman, Crystal
    1910   *Work Accidents and the Law.* New York: Sage Foundation, Charities Publication Committee.

Ehrenberg, Ronald G., and Smith, Robert S.
    1985   *Modern Labor Economics: Theory and Public Policy.* 2d ed. Glenview, Ill.: Scott, Foresman.

Einhorn, Hillel J., and Hogarth, Robin M.
    1981   "Behavioral Decision Theory: Processes of Judgment and Choice." *Annual Review of Psychology* 32(1981):53–88.

Employers' Liability Commission for the State of Illinois
    1910   *Report of the Employers' Liability Commission for the State of Illinois.* Chicago: Stromberg, Allen.

Falk, I. S.
    1936   *Security against Sickness.* Garden City: Doubleday, Doran.
    1937   "Memorandum F" (June 23, 1937). Record Group 47. Records of the Social Security Administration. Chairman's Files, 056.11–056.12. National Archives.

Fenn, Paul
    1981   "Sickness Duration, Residual Disability, and Income Replacement: An Empirical Analysis." *Economic Journal* (March 1981): 158–73.

Flanigan, Robert J., and Mitchell, Daniel J. B.
    1982   "Wage Determination and Public Policy." In *Industrial Relations Research in the 1970s: Review and Appraisal,* edited by Thomas A. Kochan, Daniel J. B. Mitchell, and Lee Dyer, 45–94. Madison, Wis.: Industrial Relations Research Association.

Flinn, C., and Heckman, J.
    1982   "Models for the Analysis of Labor Force Dynamics." In *Advances in Econometrics,* edited by R. Basmann and G. Rhodes, 1:35–95. Cambridge: Cambridge University Press.

Gersuny, Carl
    1981   *Work Hazards and Industrial Conflict.* Hanover, N.H.: University Press of New England.

Grether, David M., and Plott, Charles R.
    1979   "Economic Theory of Choice and the Preference Reversal Phenomena." *American Economic Review* 69, 4(September 1979):623–38.

Griliches, Zvi
    1967   "Distributed Lags: A Survey." *Econometrica* 35 (January 1967):16–49.
Haber, William, and Murray, Merrill G.
    1966   *Unemployment Insurance in the American Economy.* Homewood, Ill.: Richard D. Irwin.
Heckman, James J., and Singer, Burton
    1982   "The Identification Problem in Econometric Models for Duration Data." In *Advances in Econometrics,* edited by W. Hildenbrand. Cambridge: Cambridge University Press.
    1984   "A Method for Minimizing the Impact of Distributional Assumptions in Econometric Models for Duration Data." *Econometrica* 52(March 1984):271–320.
Hirschman, Albert O.
    1965   "Obstacles to Development: A Classification and a Quasi-Vanishing Act." *Economic Development and Cultural Change* 13(July 1965):385–93.
Industrial Relations Counselors
    1958   *Utilization of the Physically Handicapped Worker—A Pilot Study of Management Experience* (April 1958). New York.
Interagency Task Force on Workplace Safety and Health
    1978   *Making Prevention Pay: Draft Final Report.* December 1978. Washington D.C. (Mimeo.)
Interdepartmental Workers' Compensation Task Force
    1977   *Workers' Compensation: Is There a Better Way?* January 1977. Washington, D.C. (Mimeo.)
Jennings, D.; Amabile, T. M.; and Ross L.
    1980   "Informal Covariation Assessment: Data-Based vs. Theory-Based Judgments." In *Judgments under Uncertainty: Heuristics and Biases,* edited by Amos Tversky, Daniel Kahneman, and Paul Slovic. New York: Cambridge University Press.
Johnson, William G.
    1983   "Work Disincentives of Benefit Payments." In *Safety and the Work Force: Incentives and Disincentives in Workers' Compensation,* edited by John D. Worrall. Ithaca, N.Y.: ILR Press.
Joseph, Lawrence
    1983   "The Causation Issue in Workers' Compensation Mental Disability Cases: An Analysis, Solutions, and a Perspective." 36 *Vanderbilt Law Review* 263(March 1983).
Kahneman, Daniel, and Tversky, Amos
    1979   "Prospect Theory: An Analysis of Decisions under Risk." *Econometrica* 47, 2(March 1979):263–91.
    1982   "Intuitive Prediction: Biases and Corrective Procedures." *Management Science.*

Katona, George
    1951   *Psychological Analysis of Economic Behavior.* New York: McGraw-Hill.

Kessler, Henry
    1949   *IAIABC Proceedings.* Washington, D.C.: 168.

Kiefer, Nick M., and Neuman, George R.
    1979   "An Empirical Job-Search Model, with a Test of the Constant Reservation Wage Hypothesis." *Journal of Political Economy* 87 (February 1979):89–108.

Kunreuther, Howard
    1978   *Disaster Insurance Protection: Public Policy Lessons.* New York: Wiley and Sons.

Lancaster, T.
    1979   "Econometric Methods for the Duration of Unemployment." *Econometrica* 47(1979):939–56.

Larson, Arthur
    1978   *The Laws of Workmen's Compensation* (originally published in 1952). 4 vols. and cumulative supplement. New York: Matthew Bender.
    1982   "The Current Status of the Compensation Exclusivity Doctrine." Paper Presented at the NCCI Seminar on Workers' Compensation Current Trends. New York City, November 1982.

Larson, Lloyd W.
    1973   "The Role of Subsequent-Injury Funds in Encouraging Employment of Handicapped Workers." In *Supplemental Studies for the National Commission on State Workmen's Compensation Laws,* National Commission on State Workmen's Compensation Laws, vol. 2. Washington, D.C.: Government Printing Office.
    1979   *Analysis of Current Laws Reflecting Worker Benefits for Occupational Diseases.* Report prepared for the U.S. Department of Labor.

Larson, Lloyd W., and Burton, John F., Jr.
    1981   *Special Funds in Workers' Compensation.* Report prepared for the Employment Standards Administration, U.S. Department of Labor.

Leigh, J. Paul
    1982   "Are Unionized Blue Collar Jobs More Hazardous than Non-Unionized Blue Collar Jobs?" *Journal of Labor Research* 3(Summer 1982):349–57.

McAuley, Robert
    1982   Letter to R. B. Victor. December 21, 1982.

McDonald, James B.
    1984   "Some Generalized Functions for the Size Distribution of Income." *Econometrica* 52 (May 1984): 647–64.

McGraw-Hill
    Annual Survey of Investment in Employee Safety and Health.
Martin, George
    1976   *Madam Secretary: Frances Perkins.* Boston: Houghton Mifflin.
Meyers, Robert J.
    1981   *Social Security.* 2d ed. Homewood, Ill.: Richard D. Irwin.
Millis, Harry A., and Montgomery, Royal E.
    1938   *Labor's Risks and Social Insurance.* New York: McGraw-Hill.
"Minutes of the Advisory Council Meeting." October 21–22, 1938. RG 47,
    Records of the Executive Director, File 025, Box 138, National
    Archives.
Mitchell, Olivia S.
    1982   "The Labor Market Impact of Federal Regulation: OSHA,
    ERISA, EEO, and Minimum Wage." In *Industrial Relations Re-
    search in the 1970s: Review and Appraisal,* edited by Thomas A.
    Kochan, Daniel J. B. Mitchell, and Lee Dyer, 149–86. Madison,
    Wis.: Industrial Relations Research Association.
Naples, Michelle I., and Gordon, David M.
    1981   "The Industrial Accident Rate: Creating a Consistent Time
    Series." (Mimeo.)
National Archives
    RG 174. Records of the Department of Labor. Mitchell. Files
    of Arthur Larson. Michael J. Quill to Dwight D. Eisenhower,
    December 14, 1953; Arthur Larson to James Mitchell, August
    9, 1954; Clara Beyer to Mr. Gilhooley, January 25, 1954.
National Commission on State Workmen's Compensation Laws
    1972   *The Report of the National Commission on State Workmen's Com-
    pensation Laws.* Washington, D.C.: Government Printing Office.
    1973   *Compendium of Workmen's Compensation.* Washington, D.C.: Gov-
    ernment Printing Office.
National Council on Compensation Insurance
    1981a *ABC's of Experience Rating.* New York: NCCI.
    1981b *The Pricing of Worker's Compensation Insurance.* New York: NCCI.
    1982   *An Indepth View of Experience Rating.* New York: NCCI.
Nelson, Daniel
    1969   *Unemployment Insurance: The American Experience.* Madison: Uni-
    versity of Wisconsin Press.
Nisbett, R. E., and Ross, L.
    1980   *Human Inference: Strategies and Shortcomings of Social Judgments.*
    Englewood Cliffs, N.J.: Prentice-Hall.
Nisbett, R. E.; Zukier, Henry; and Lemley, Ronald E.
    1981   "The Dilution Effect: Nondiagnostic Information Weakens the
    Implications of Diagnostic Information." *Cognitive Psychology*
    13(1981):248–77.

Oi, Walter Y.
  1973   "Workmen's Compensation and Industrial Safety." In *Supplemental Studies for the National Commission on State Workmen's Compensation Laws,* vol. 1. Washington, D.C.: Government Printing Office.
  1974   "On the Economics of Industrial Safety." *Law and Contemporary Problems.*
Olson, Craig A.
  1981   "An Analysis of Wage Differentials Received by Workers on Dangerous Jobs." *Journal of Human Resources* 16, 2 (Spring 1981):167–85.
OSHA
  1970   PL 91–596.
  1979   "OSHA Report Number SP03." May 22, 1979. (Mimeo.)
Peltzman, Sam
  1976   "Towards a More General Theory of Regulation." *Journal of Law and Economics* 19, 2(August 1976):211–40.
Perloff, Jeffrey M., and Salop, Steven C.
  1980   "Firm-Specific Information Product Differentiation and Industry Equilibrium." University of Pennsylvania and F.T.C., April 1980. (Mimeo.)
Posner, Richard A.
  1972   "A Theory of Negligence." *Journal of Legal Studies* (January 1972): 44–95.
Price, Daniel N.
  1979   "Workers' Compensation Programs in the 1970s." *Social Security Bulletin* 42, 5(May 1979):3–24.
  1980   "Workers' Compensation: 1978 Program Update." *Social Security Bulletin* 43, 10(October 1980):3–10.
  1981   "Workers' Compensation Coverage, Benefits, and Costs, 1979." *Social Security Bulletin* 44, 9(October 1980):9–13.
Ream, Donald L.
  1966   "Workmen's Compensation as It Applies in the United States." In *1966 Convention Proceedings of IAIABC,* International Association of Industrial Accident Boards and Commissions.
Reede, Arthur H.
  1947   *Adequacy of Workmen's Compensation.* Cambridge, Mass.: Harvard University Press.
"Rehabilitation Committee Report." *154 IAIABC Proceedings.* Washington, D.C.: 24–25.
Ross, L.
  1977   "The Intuitive Psychologist and His Shortcomings." In *Advances in Experimental Social Psychology,* edited by L. Berkowitz, vol. 10. New York: Academic Press.

Rubinow, Isaac
　　1934　*The Quest for Security*. New York: Henry Holt.
Ruser, John W.
　　1984　"Workers' Compensation Insurance, Experience Rating and Occupational Injuries." Office of Research and Evaluation, U.S. Bureau of Labor Statistics. Washington, D.C. June. (Mimeo.)
Russell, L. B.
　　1973　"Pricing Industrial Accidents." In *Supplemental Studies for the National Commission on State Workmen's Compensation Laws*, vol. 3, National Commission on State Workmen's Compensation Laws. Washington, D.C.: Government Printing Office.
　　1974　"Safety Incentives in Workers' Compensation." *Journal of Human Resources* 9, 3(Summer 1974):361.
Simon, Herbert A.
　　1955　"A Behavioral Model of Rational Choice." *Quarterly Journal of Economics* 69 (February 1955):99–118.
Slovic, Paul; Fischhoff, Baruch; Lichtenstein, Sarah
　　1976　"The Certainty Illusion." *ORI Research Bulletin* 16, 4 (1976).
　　1977　"Behavioral Decision Theory." *Annual Review of Psychology* 28(1977):1–39.
Smith, Robert S.
　　1979　"Compensating Wage Differentials and Public Policy: A Review." *Industrial and Labor Relations Review* 32, 3 (April 1979): 339–52.
Somers, Herbert M., and Somers, Anne R.
　　1954　*Workmen's Compensation: Prevention Insurance and Rehabilitation of Occupational Disability*. New York: Wiley and Sons.
Staten, Michael, and Umbeck, John
　　1982　"Information Costs and the Incentive to Shirk: Disability Compensation of Air Traffic Controllers." *American Economic Review* 72, 5:1023–37.
　　1983　"Compensating Stress-Induced Disability: Disincentive Problems." In *Safety and the Work Force: Incentives and Disincentives in Workers' Compensation*, edited by John D. Worrall, 103–27. Ithaca, N.Y.: ILR Press.
Stigler, George J.
　　1971　"The Theory of Economic Regulation." *Bell Journal of Economics* (Spring 1971).
Tinsley, La Verne C.
　　1982　"Workers' Compensation: Key Legislation in 1981." *Monthly Labor Review* 105, 2 (February 1982):24–30.
Tversky, Amos, and Kahneman, Daniel
　　1974　"Judgment under Uncertainty: Heuristics and Biases." *Science* 185(1974):1124–31.
U.S. Bureau of the Census
　　Annual Survey of Manufacturers.

U.S. Chamber of Commerce
  1982 *Analysis of Workers' Compensation Laws, 1982.* Washington, D.C.: Chamber of Commerce.
U.S. Congress, Senate
  1914 *Workmen's Compensation—Report upon Operation of State Laws.* 63d Cong., 2d sess. Doc. 416. Washington, D.C.: Government Printing Office.
U.S. Department of Labor
  1982 *Monthly Labor Review* 105, 4(April 1982).
U.S. Department of Labor, Bureau of Labor Standards
  1961 *Workmen's Compensation and the Physically Handicapped Worker.* Bulletin 234. Washington, D.C.: Government Printing Office.
U.S. Department of Labor, Bureau of Statistics
  1974–82 *Occupational Injuries and Illnesses in the United States by Industry.* Washington, D.C.: Government Printing Office.
U.S. Department of Labor, ESA-OWCP
  1969 *State Workers' Compensation Laws.* Bulletin 161. Rev. ed. Washington, D.C.: U.S. Department of Labor Wage and Labor Standards Administration.
  1981 *State Compliance with the 19 Essential Recommendations of the National Commission on State Workmen's Compensation Laws, 1972–1980.* Washington, D.C.: Government Printing Office.
  1982 *State Workers' Compensation Laws.* Washington, D.C.: Government Printing Office.
  1983 *State Workers' Compensation Laws.* Washington, D.C.: Government Printing Office.
  n.d. "State Workers' Compensation Laws in Effect on April 1, 1983 Compared with the National Commission on State Workmen's Compensation Laws." (Mimeo.)
U.S. Departments of Labor; Commerce; Health, Education, and Welfare; Housing and Urban Development
  1974 *White Paper on Workers' Compensation.* Washington, D.C.: Government Printing Office.
Van Doren, D. H.
  1981 *Workmen's Compensation and Insurance.* New York: Moffat, Ward.
Victor, R. B.
  1983 *Workers' Compensation and Workplace Safety: The Nature of Employer Financial Incentives.* Santa Monica, Calif. The Rand Corporation, R-2979-ICJ. January 1983.
Viscusi, W. Kip
  1979a *Employment Hazards: An Investigation of Market Performance.* Cambridge, Mass.: Harvard University Press.
  1979b "The Impact of Occupational Safety and Health Regulation." *Bell Journal of Economics* 10, 1(Spring 1979):117–40.

1979c "Job Hazards and Worker Quit Rates: An Analysis of Adaptive Worker Behavior." *International Economic Review* 20, 1(February 1979):29–58.

1980a "Imperfect Job Risk Information and Optimal Workmen's Compensation Benefits." *Journal of Public Economics* 14 (1980):319–37.

1980b "A Theory of Job Shopping: A Bayesian Perspective." *Quarterly Journal of Economics* 94, 3(May 1980): 609:14.

1980c "Union, Labor Market Structure, and the Welfare Implications of the Quality of Work." *Journal of Labor Research* 1, 1(Spring 1980):175–92.

Weber, Robert J.
1982 "The Allais Paradox, Dutch Auctions and Alpha-Utility." Northwestern University. (Mimeo.)

Weidenbaum, Murray L., and de Fina, Robert
1978 "The Cost of Federal Regulation of Economic Activity." American Enterprise Institute reprint, no. 88, May 1978.

Weiss, Harry
1918–35 "Employer Liability and Workmen's Compensation." In *A History of Labor Legislation in the United States*, John R. Commons et al., 4 vols. New York: Macmillan.

Wiebe, Robert
1962 *Businessmen and Reform.* Cambridge, Mass.: Harvard University Press.

Williams, C. Arthur, Jr.; Turnbull, J. G.; and Cheit, E. F.
1971 "Rehabilitation of Disabled Workers and Employment of the Handicapped." *Report of the National Workshop on Rehabilitation and Workmen's Compensation.* Washington, D.C.: National Institute on Rehabilitation and Health Services.

1982 *Economic and Social Security.* 5th ed. New York: Wiley and Sons.

Woodward, Edward C.
1984 "Remarks before the U.S. Senate Subcommittee on Labor."

Worrall, John D.
1982 "Overlapping Benefits: Workers' Compensation and Other Income Sources." National Council on Compensation Insurance. November 1982. (Mimeo.)

1983 ed., *Safety and the Work Force: Incentives and Disincentives in Workers' Compensation Insurance.* Ithaca, N.Y.: ILR Press.

Worrall, John D., and Appel, David
1982 "The Wage Replacement Rate and Benefit Utilization in Workers' Compensation Insurance." *Journal of Risk and Insurance* 49, 3(September 1982):361–71.

Worrall, John D., and Butler, Richard J.
1983 "Health Conditions and Job Hazards: Union and Nonunion Jobs." *Journal of Labor Research* 4(Fall 1983): 339–47.

INDEX

CONTRIBUTORS

David Appel is assistant vice president of the National Council on Compensation Insurance (NCCI). He received his Ph.D. from Rutgers University, where he also taught before joining NCCI. Mr. Appel has written extensively on workers' compensation insurance and testified frequently in regulatory hearings. His work has appeared in the *Journal of Risk and Insurance* and the *Journal of Insurance Regulation*.

Ann P. Bartel is an associate professor at Columbia University, where she received her Ph.D. Ms. Bartel has written a number of articles for such publications as *Industrial and Labor Relations Review, Review of Economics and Statistics*, and the *Journal of Law and Economics*.

Edward Berkowitz is an associate professor of history and director, Program in History and Public Policy at George Washington University. He received his Ph.D. from Northwestern University. Among Mr. Berkowitz's published works is *Creating the Welfare State: The Political Economy of Twentieth Century Reform* with Kim McQuaid. He is editor of *Disability Programs and Government Policies*. Mr. Berkowitz has published articles in the *Journal of Economic History, Social Services Review*, and the *Historians*, among others.

Monroe Berkowitz is a professor in the Department of Economics and director of the Bureau of Economic Research for Rutgers University, New Brunswick, New Jersey. Mr. Berkowitz received his Ph.D. from Columbia University. He was editor of Supplemental Studies on Workmen's Compensation, National Commission on State Workmen's Compensation Laws. Mr. Berkowitz has written numerous books and articles on workers compensation and disability economics.

John F. Burton, Jr. is a professor in the Department of Labor Economics and Collective Bargaining, Labor Law and Labor History at the New York State School of Industrial and Labor Relations, Cornell University. He received his LL.B. and Ph.D. in 1965 from the University of Michigan. He was chairman of the National Commission on State Workmen's Compensation Laws, 1971–72, and has published dozens of articles on workers' compensation insurance.

Richard J. Butler is an assistant professor, Department of Economics, at Brigham Young University. He received his Ph.D. in 1979 from the Department of Economics at the University of Chicago. He has published papers in the *Southern Economic Journal, Industrial and Labor Relations Review, Journal of Human Resources, Review of Economics and Statistics*, and *Economic Journal*.

William T. Dickens is an assistant professor of economics and a research affiliate of the Group for the Applications of Mathematics and Statistics to Economics and of the Institute for Industrial Relations at the University of California, Berkeley. Professor Dickens graduated from MIT in 1980 with a Ph.D. in economics. He has published articles on occupational safety and health, labor productivity, union representation elections, and other industrial relations topics. His work has appeared in the *American Economic Review*.

Lloyd W. Larson is retired from the post of research associate, New York State School of Industrial and Labor Relations, Cornell University. Mr. Larson received his B.A. and M.A. degrees from the University of Minnesota and did further graduate work at George Washington University and the University of Minnesota. He is author of "Changing Concepts in Workmen's Compensation Coverage," published in *Report of a Workshop Sponsored by the National Institutes on Rehabilitation and Health Services, 1971*.

Lacy Glenn Thomas is an assistant professor at Columbia University, Graduate School of Business. He received his Ph.D. from Duke University. Mr. Thomas has published in the *Journal of Law and Economics, Quarterly Journal of Economics* and the *American Economic Review*.

Richard B. Victor is executive director of the Workers Compensation Research Institute in Cambridge, Massachusetts. He was formerly an economist with the Rand Corporation–Institute for Civil Justice, where he specialized in workplace and environmental regulation and liability. Dr. Victor received his Ph.D. and J.D. degrees from the University of Michigan.

C. Arthur Williams, Jr. is a professor at the School of Management, University of Minnesota. Mr. Williams received his Ph.D. in Business Administration from Columbia University. He is currently editor of the *Journal of Risk and Insurance* and sits on the board of directors for St. Paul Companies, Inc. since 1975. In 1977–78 he was vice chairman, Minnesota Workers' Compensation Study Commission. Mr. Williams has published numerous articles and books, including *Economic and Social Security* with J. G. Turnbill and E. F. Cheit, and *Insurance Arrangements under Workers' Compensation* with P. S. Barth.

John D. Worrall is associate professor of economics at Rutgers University. He is a former vice president of the National Council on Compensation Insurance (NCCI). He received his Ph.D. from Rutgers University. The editor of *Safety and the Work Force* (ILR Press), he has published many articles on workers' compensation and disability policy, including work in the *Journal of Human Resources, Journal of Risk and Insurance, Review of Economics and Statistics*, and *The Economic Journal*.

A worker who suffers a job-related injury receives benefits determined under a state insurance system. In this volume of essays, twelve economists and social scientists consider whether the various schemes that comprise the workers' compensation system function as intended. Do they replace an adequate portion of earnings without providing so much income as to discourage a worker from returning to the job? How do the benefits compare with those received by other workers with comparable disabilities? How much time and money are consumed by the insurance procedures themselves?

The question of how to apportion risk efficiently between the employer and the employee is central to these studies. The authors examine possible trade-offs and analyze the results of such cost-allocation schemes as experience-rating and special funds.

In addition, a number of the authors discuss new pressures on the workers' compensation system generated by the Occupational Safety and Health Act and by the rise in claims related to occupational disease.

The studies here have clear implications for the management of social insurance. They should be read by anyone involved in formulating or administering policy, insurance and benefit professionals, and economists.

John D. Worrall teaches economics at Rutgers University, where he is affiliated with the Bureau of Economic Research.

David Appel is assistant vice president, economic and social research, of the National Council on Compensation Insurance.